N/Menzies|£7.95

THE
SEAFOOD KITCHEN

THE
SEAFOOD KITCHEN

Judy Ridgway

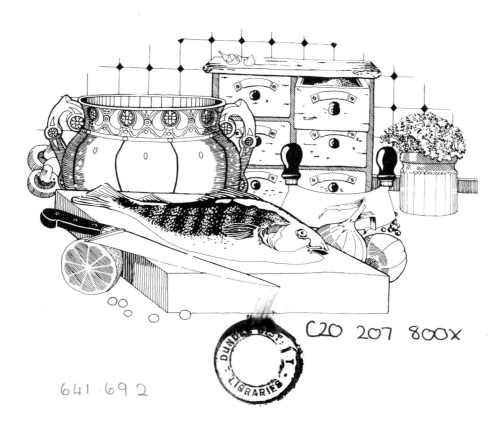

Ward Lock Limited · London

First published in Great Britain in 1981
by Ward Lock Limited, 47 Marylebone Lane,
London W1M 6AX, a Pentos Company.

Layout by Charlotte Westbrook

Text filmset in Plantin
by Brown Knight and Truscott Limited

Printed and bound in Great Britain by R.J. Acford Limited, Chichester

British Library Cataloguing in Publication Data

Ridgway, Judy
  Seafood kitchen.
  1. Cookery (Fish)
  I. Title
  641.6'9'2   TX747
  ISBN 0-7063-5992-5

Contents

Acknowledgements

Photography by Edmund Goldspink
Line drawings in fish chart by Sue Sharples
Other line drawings by Gérard Roadley-Battin
Photographs on pages 116 and 130 were supplied
courtesy of Alcan Polyfoil and John West Foods respectively
The author would also like to thank the White Fish Authority
for their help

Notes

It is important to follow *either* the metric *or* the imperial
measures when using the recipes in this book. Where canned
foods are used, the undrained weight is given. All spoon
measures are level.
When flour is called for, use plain flour.
Each dish will serve 4 people.

Introduction

Fish is one of my favourite foods. I choose it in restaurants far more often than any other kind of dish and it appears regularly on my table at home. I suppose that part of my liking for fish rests on early memories of my mother's home cooking and she was certainly never guilty of serving overcooked or dried-up fish. But it also rests on a fascination with the huge variety of interesting shapes, colours and textures offered by the fish and shellfish which are available to us.

I never miss the chance to visit a seaside fish market or to talk to one of the diminishing band of high street fishmongers. The highlight of a visit to Brittany was seeing the rows and rows of stalls at the Lorient fish market all heaving with mountains of live shellfish. For me, holidays abroad are always times to experiment and some of my favourite dishes have come from eating at the local bars and restaurants and begging the chef to let me into the secret or trying to work out and test the recipes afterwards.

Of course not all foreign fish is available in Britain but methods of cooking, flavourings, sauces and garnishes can all be adapted to suit our own fish. Charcoal-grilled sardines from the Algarve, fish soups from the South of France, chowders from New England and tuna recipes from South Africa have all found their way into this book.

It never ceases to amaze me that despite the many exciting possibilities there seem to be thousands of cooks who never think of serving fish. In the past, fish was served far more often. This was probably due both to religious considerations and to economic ones. The early Christian church gradually extended the custom of eating fish on Fridays to include Wednesdays, Saturdays and the whole of Lent. Though thanks to a strange view held of their biological origins the barnacle goose, the puffin and the beaver's tail were excluded from the ban on meat and classified as fish!

By Elizabethan times religious observance of fast days was declining but meat was still in short supply. The Queen therefore passed a law enforcing the three meatless days. Perhaps the English dislike of compulsion has contributed to the general unpopularity of fish. However, all this fish eating did mean that a very respectable fish cuisine was built up and both medieval

and Elizabethan cooks were far more adventurous in their use of fish than we are today. They used all kinds of fish in spicy soups and stews, large baked pies and even in blancmanges and jellies. Some of the recipes for these have survived to the present day and they are well worth trying. My recipes for Jellied Eels, Soused Herrings, Baked Stuffed Bream and Poached Mackerel with Lemon and Gooseberry Sauce are all based on recipes from the past.

However, I did draw the line at the Cornish Stargazy Pie which has whole fresh pilchards or herrings arranged so that their heads are left poking out through the pie crust to gaze at the stars. Nor can I regret the passing of the 18th century passion for green oysters, which were gathered in September from the estuaries of Essex. These oysters developed a growth of harmless green algae and were eagerly sought after.

Oysters were widely thought to be an aphrodisiac and since they were available in large quantities there was no lack of gentlemen keen to test the truth of this assertion. Fish was also held to be good for the brain but this could well have been a nursery tale designed to get reluctant children to eat up. Today there seems to be a fear that fish can't compare nutritionally with good red meat. In fact a cod steak contains just about the same amount of protein as a beef steak of the same weight and it is much easier to digest.

I have often asked my friends why, when we are a nation of anglers and surrounded by sea, we don't serve fish more often. Some respond by mentioning a fear of bones, but there are lots of fish which are not particularly bony and nearly all frozen fish is sold ready boned and filleted.

Others refer to the high price of fish but fish is no more expensive than meat and some of the more recently marketed varieties like huss and coley are extremely economical. Yet others say that they don't like fish because it is dry and tasteless and it is here, I think, that the problem really lies. Too often fish is overcooked, the sauce is lumpy and tasteless and it is not surprising that people are put off.

In writing this book I have tried to show that cooking fish successfully is not difficult and that the results are well worth the care and attention that the enthusiastic cook gives to preparing other kinds of food. I have also included some guidelines for dealing with fish caught by the anglers of the family or bought at the quayside.

My own passion for fish has led to all sorts of culinary experiences, though none so bizarre as the green oysters of the 18th century, and I sincerely hope that this book will tempt others to try their hand at producing many more fish feasts.

Judy Ridgway

1 Choice and Selection

The choice of fish and shellfish available to the cook is as wide, if not wider, than it has ever been and this is true despite some shortages caused by over-fishing and the general decline of the British fishing industry. As well as the traditionally popular fish such as cod, plaice and haddock, the fishmonger's slab has gained new and perhaps unfamiliar fish like coley, grey mullet, huss and monkfish. Added to these are freshwater carp, salmon, trout and bream and all the different kinds of shellfish. The result is a wide array of fish that can be used in a multitude of dishes.

Fish and shellfish are also widely available either frozen or canned and in some instances in pre-packed, unprocessed form at supermarkets and large grocers. And many delicatessens sell salted, smoked and pickled fish.

Flat and Round Fish

Fish are known as flat fish or round fish but this classification has little value to the cook except that it may give an indication of the form in which the fishmonger is likely to sell it. Flat fish such as plaice, for example, are usually filleted or sold whole. Round fish like hake will be cut into steaks across the body, and mackerel and herring will probably be sold whole. However, both mackerel and herring can be sold filleted and large flat fish are often cut into steaks. In addition some fish are so large that the fishmonger tends to display them skinned and cut into conveniently sized portions.

White and Oily Fish

A more important distinction is between white fish and oily fish. The milder tasting white fish such as plaice, cod and sole store their natural oils in the liver but in oily or fatty fish this oil is distributed throughout the body tissues to give a much stronger flavoured fish. As a rule oily fish such as salmon, mackerel and herring are preferred for grilling and baking as their fat content helps to stop them drying up. But, of course, white fish can also be cooked in this way if it is well basted.

Lean white fish poaches and steams well as the flesh is firm with little tendency to fall apart. However, salmon also takes well to these methods of cooking. In fact all fish can actually be cooked by any of the basic processes outlined in Chapter 3 provided that care is taken to allow for its particular characteristics.

Some freshwater fish is sold at the fishmonger and it is important to know if it is a mud dweller or not. If it is, the fish should be soaked in salted water for a few hours before cooking. This will help to remove the rather muddy flavour that can pervade the flesh of some of these fish. Fish to treat in this way are carp and bream bought at the fishmonger and tench or pike brought home by the angler. Incidentally, fishing for the table is best done in streams and rivers rather than in small lakes or ponds, which are likely to be muddier.

Shellfish is usually sold ready cooked though bivalves such as cockles and mussels are sold raw and must be cooked as soon as they are taken home. Oysters are also sold raw and can be eaten that way or cooked. Uncooked crabs and lobsters can be bought at some seaside markets and these, too, should be cooked as soon as possible after purchase.

Nutritional Value of Fish

Fish is an extremely nutritious food. It contains a very high proportion of usable protein. And most fish are carbohydrate free.

White fish contain little or no fat in the flesh but oily fish can contain as much as 30 per cent fat. This fat is high in polyunsaturated fatty acids. The total fat content will depend upon the species. Herring, for example, contains about twice as much fat as salmon. The fat content also depends upon the time of year. Oily fish are generally fattest in the late summer and early autumn and leanest after spawning in early summer.

Shellfish contain twice as much salt as other fish, a little carbohydrate and about the same protein and fat content as white fish.

Minerals and vitamins present in all fish include phosphorous, calcium and the vitamin B complex. Sea fish are important for their iodine content and this is particularly true of herrings and sardines. Oily fish are a good source of vitamins A, D and E and some shellfish are rich in iron. Some of these minerals and vitamins leach out when the fish is cooked but provided that the cooking liquor is used for soups or sauces they will not be wasted.

Freezing fish causes no loss in nutritional value though some vitamin B is lost into the drip on thawing. This can be avoided by cooking small pieces of fish straight from the freezer. Canning causes a loss of part of the vitamin B complex but most of the other nutrients remain stable throughout the canning process.

Provided that they are not fried in batter or drowned in butter, white fish and shellfish are excellent foods for the slimmer. And because white fish has no connective tissue, it is very easily digested and therefore widely used in invalid cooking.

Calorie Content of Common Fish

Type of fish	Cals. per 100g/4oz fish
Dabs and Flounders	80
Oysters	80
Cod	82
Mussels	87
Scallops	88
Lemon Sole	90
Whiting	90
Plaice	92
Cockles	95
Coley and Pollack	95
Haddock	95
Hake	95
Squid	97
Trout	100
Turbot	100
Dover Sole	106
Skate	110
Smoked Haddock	110
Shrimps	114
Brill	115
Prawns	120
Crab	127
Grey Mullet	130
Halibut	130
Lobster	130
Cod Roe	150
Mackerel	180
Herring	182
Canned Sardines	190
Canned Salmon	210
Kippers	230
Canned Pilchards	234
Canned Tuna	236

Cost and Availability

The price of fish and shellfish varies quite substantially, both according to the type of fish and the season. Some fish which

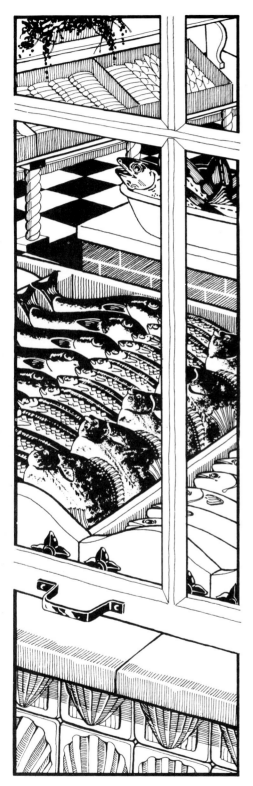

were extremely plentiful in the past have now become luxury items and other cheaper and more plentiful fish have been introduced in their place.

Contrary to popular belief fish does not have to be expensive and some varieties can be bought at local markets for as little as 50-60p per 450g/1lb. Others, in the luxury class, can cost anything upwards of £3 per 450g/1lb. The majority, of course, fall somewhere between these extremes.

To help the budget-conscious, I have arranged the fish recipes in this book according to cost. Each chapter begins with the most economical dishes and progresses to the most expensive. A general indication of the price of fish currently available is given in the charts at the end of this chapter, but this is only intended as an outline guide. Prices could change again if the fishing grounds are over-fished and prices vary quite considerably with the season and the type of cut being offered.

On the latter point it is worth remembering that in general a whole fish will lose about half its weight when it is headed, tailed and boned. Fillets and steaks therefore will cost correspondingly more for their weight than whole fish.

Everyone knows that salmon is only caught at certain times of the year but in fact all fish are subject to some seasonal fluctuations either because of quality variations or because of closed seasons which allow the fish to reproduce and grow undisturbed and thus provide for the coming seasons.

The various methods of preserving fish have traditionally extended the choice at any one time of the year, though the end result in some cases may not taste very much like the fresh original. However, salted, smoked and even some canned fish have become delicacies in their own right. And the advent of commercial freezing has meant that many seasonal fish and shellfish are now available all the year round in a form virtually indistinguishable from the original.

Choosing Fresh Fish

Unprocessed fish straight from the sea, river or fish farm is referred to as wet fish. It should be really fresh and should be cooked the day that it is bought. One reason why fish is unpopular with some people could be the fear that it has 'gone off'. The texture and flavour of fish which is a few days old is quite different from the succulent feel and fine flavour of really fresh fish.

With modern methods of transportation, fish on the inland fishmonger's slab should be almost as fresh as that sold at the seaside and it is certainly not in the fishmonger's interests to sell stale fish. However, if you are not sure of your fishmonger, your eyes and nose can provide you with all the information you need.

Here are the points to look for:

· The fish should have a fresh saline smell, not too fishy nor smelling of ammonia

· The flesh should be firm and springy to the touch. Avoid fish with droopy tails. Test the flesh with your fingers. If an imprint remains after the fish has been handled the fish is not fresh

· Choose fish that are bright in colour—all fish loses its brilliancy with age. Look at the dark side of flat fish, for this side shows age first: instead of being bright and shiny it becomes dull

· The eyes should be bright and bulging. Avoid fish with dull and sunken eyes

· The gills of most fish should be red

· For smoked fish check that the skin is dry and has a bright and healthy bloom. Avoid fish whose skin is damp or slimy

· When buying fillets or steaks look for firm, translucent flesh and avoid any that have a yellowish tinge to them

For advice on choosing shellfish, refer to the chart on **pages 32-36**.

How Much to Buy

The question of how much to buy is sometimes a problem for those cooks who are unfamiliar with fish. The answer will of course depend on the particular type of fish you have chosen but here is a general guide to quantities per person.

White fish	Whole fish ungutted with head	300g/10oz
	Whole fish gutted with head	225g/8oz
	Steaks and fillets	175g/6oz
Oily fish	Whole fish ungutted with head	225g/8oz
	Whole fish gutted with head	200g/7oz
	Steaks	175g/6oz
	Fillets	150g/5oz
Shellfish	Prawns in their shells	300ml/½pint
	Shelled prawns	100g/4oz
	Lobster	½-1 per person
	Crab	½-1 per person

Processed Fish

Of course, not all fish is sold at the fishmonger. Much of it is processed by one means or another and sold in a form that will keep for some length of time.

Commercially Frozen Fish

Very often frozen fish is cleaned and frozen on the same day that it is caught which means that it is as fresh, if not fresher, than wet fish sold in the markets. It is usually sold as fillets or steaks and thus avoids all fuss and mess, but whole fish are also available. The choice ranges from cod, haddock, plaice and coley fillets to whole trout and salmon. Smoked fish is also sold frozen and this includes mackerel, haddock and kippers. A wide selection of cooked shellfish is also available frozen, including dressed crabs, prawns (both peeled and unpeeled) and scallops.

The current trend among frozen food manufacturers is to offer fish that is not only skinned, boned and filleted but also ready prepared for instant cooking. The fillets are coated in breadcrumbs or batter or are sealed in a cook-in bag with sauce.

Whichever you choose, make sure that the pack is in good condition and has not been stored for a long time. Avoid solid packets which are beginning to soften at the edges.

Canned Fish

Oily fish such as herring, salmon, tuna, mackerel and sardines all take well to canning and a number of manufacturers offer these and other fish in natural brine, oil or sauce. Shellfish are also suitable candidates for canning, and here the choice ranges from crab, lobster and shrimps to mussels, oysters and clams. Avoid cans which are dented or which are beginning to rust.

Salted Fish

This is prepared by soaking the fish in brine or by dry salting. Fish such as cod, hake, haddock and herrings are salted by packing in dry salt after gutting. Salt cod is popular in Spain and Portugal but is fairly rare in Britain.

Smoked Fish

This is either hot smoked, in which case it is fully cooked, or cold smoked, which means that further cooking is required. The choice of hot smoked fish includes small haddock (smokies), herring (buckling), trout, mackerel and sprats. Haddock and herring are also cold smoked, as are salmon, cod and whiting.

Herrings are cold smoked either whole and ungutted (bloaters) or split and gutted (kippers). With the exception of smoked salmon, which is eaten raw, cold smoked fish should be poached in water or milk, grilled or used in made dishes.

Pickled Fish

Fish such as herrings are commercially pickled by marinating in spiced vinegar. Rollmops are rolled with chopped onions, gherkins and peppercorns and Bismarcks are flat fillets covered with thin slices of onion. Both Bismarcks and rollmops are sold loose in delicatessens, or bottled in jars.

Storing Fish

Once wet fish has been bought it should be used as quickly as possible. If, however, it has to be stored overnight, it should be cleaned, washed and dried and placed in a covered container in the fridge. Never leave fish in its original wrappings and always make sure that it is well covered or the smell will pervade everything else that is stored in the fridge. A good place to store fish is in the tray immediately below the ice-making compartment. If you are not sure of the freshness of the fish, sprinkle with a little salt or lemon juice.

Commercially frozen fish should be taken home as quickly as possible after purchase and placed in the freezer where it will keep for up to three months. In the ice-making compartments of star-marked fridges the storage times are:- 1 star: 1 week; 2 stars: 1 month; 3 stars: 3 months.

If the fish starts to defrost on the way home, remove the fish from its wrappings and use as wet fish. Never attempt to refreeze fish that has thawed.

Frozen fish is best thawed in the fridge but it can be thawed at room temperature if it is to be used at once. Keep the drip from thawing fish for soups and sauces. Never thaw fish in water as this results in the loss of valuable nutrients.

Smoked and salted fish should be kept in the fridge and used within two or three days. Pickled and canned fish will keep until the container is opened, after which it should be eaten as soon as possible. Canned fish has a shelf life of about two years if it is packed in sauce and five years if packed in oil.

FISH		DESCRIPTION

ANCHOVIES 	★★	Small fish of the herring family with a very strong flavour
BASS 	★★	A striped fish with a large head
BREAM: SEA 	★★	A thick flat fish with deep pink skin and hard scales. The flesh is firm and white
BREAM: FRESHWATER 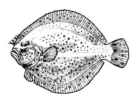	★	Freshwater bream belongs to a different species and does not have such a good flavour as sea bream
BRILL 	★★	A flat fish similar to turbot
BRISLING 	★★	Very small fish similar to sprats

STARS REFER AS FOLLOWS: *Relatively cheap fish **Medium priced fish ***Expensive fish
(In cases where fish is available in both fresh and processed forms, star rating refers to price when sold fresh.)

16

SEASONAL AVAILABILITY	PROCESSED FORMS	PREPARATION OF FRESH FISH	COOKING
–	Canned Essence	–	Use in sauces, relishes, garnishes, canapés and pasta dishes
Scarce. Best: Jan-Mar; Aug-Dec	–	Fillets	Bake
Available mainly in the South. Jun-Dec	–	Whole or fillets	Stuff and bake, grill or poach
Jul-Feb	–	Whole. Soak in mildly salted water for 3-4 hours before cooking	Stuff and bake
Available all year. Best: Sep-Mar	–	Whole or fillets	Poach, steam, grill, fry or bake. Also good served cold with mayonnaise
–	Canned Smoked	–	Use cold or in made dishes

Note: The drawings in this chart are not to scale.

FISH		DESCRIPTION

CARP

** A freshwater fish that can grow to great size. River carp has a better flavour than those bred in ponds

COD

** One of the most versatile of fish on the market, it has fairly coarse flesh and a mild flavour. It is whiter and flakier than some other white fish

COLEY (Saithe, Coalfish)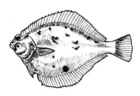

* A member of the cod family, coley has pinkish-grey flesh which turns creamy on cooking. Cooking with lemon juice helps to whiten the flesh of this and other fish

DAB

* A flat fish similar to small plaice. It has small brownish spots on dark skin

EEL: FRESHWATER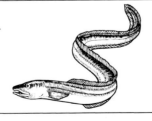

** The flesh is tender and oily

EEL: CONGER

* Grows to much greater size than the freshwater variety. The flesh is very firm and hard and needs long slow cooking

STARS REFER AS FOLLOWS: *Relatively cheap fish **Medium priced fish ***Expensive fish
(In cases where fish is available in both fresh and processed forms, star rating refers to price when sold fresh.)

SEASONAL AVAILABILITY	PROCESSED FORMS	PREPARATION OF FRESH FISH	COOKING
Jul-Feb	–	Whole. Scale and clean, and remove the 'gallstone' which lies at the back of the head or the fish will taste bitter. Soak in mildly salted water for 3-4 hours before cooking	Poach and bake. Fry small fish only
Plentiful all year. Best: Oct-Feb	Smoked Salted Frozen	Fillets and steaks. Wash and soak salted cod for 24 hours in cold water before using. Change the water from time to time	Suitable for all methods. Also for made dishes of all kinds. Good cold
Plentiful all year particularly in the North. Best: Sep-Feb	Smoked Canned Frozen	Fillets	Suitable for all methods. Also for made dishes of all kinds
Available most of the year. Best: Sep-Dec	–	Whole or fillets	Poach, steam, grill or fry
Available all year. More plentiful in the South	Smoked Jellied	Whole or steaks. Reduce oil content by removing skin before cooking	Stew or fry. Also serve cold and jellied
Apr-Aug	–	As freshwater eel	Casserole

Note: The drawings in this chart are not to scale.

FISH		DESCRIPTION

FLOUNDER		* A flat fish resembling plaice
GARFISH	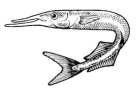	* A fish rather like a cross between a mackerel and an eel. The bones are naturally bright green in colour
GRAYLING		A freshwater fish seldom seen on the market but popular with anglers. It is similar to trout but larger
GRILSE		Very young salmon which have just left the sea to go up river for the first time. Very delicate, fine flavour
GUDGEON		A freshwater fish belonging to the carp family. They are usually about 13-15cm/5-6in in length, weighing up to 225g/8oz
GURNARD		* A low-priced fish but its bony head weighs at least one third of its total weight

STARS REFER AS FOLLOWS: *Relatively cheap fish   **Medium priced fish   ***Expensive fish
(In cases where fish is available in both fresh and processed forms, star rating refers to price when sold fresh.)

SEASONAL AVAILABILITY	PROCESSED FORMS	PREPARATION OF FRESH FISH	COOKING
Available all year. Best: Mar-Sep	–	Whole or fillets	Poach, steam, fry or grill
Scarce. Sometimes available in the South East and Wales	–	Remove the skin before cooking as this imparts a disagreeable oily taste to the fish	Poach or bake
Scarce. Best: Oct-Feb	–	Whole	Poach, grill, fry or bake
Jun-Jul	–	Whole	Poach, grill or bake. Excellent cold
Scarce in the North. Best: Jul-Feb	–	Whole, prepare as for carp	Fry or grill
Scarce except in Wales. Best: Jul-Apr	–	Whole, allow at least 450g/1lb per person	Fry, souse

Note: The drawings in this chart are not to scale.

FISH		DESCRIPTION

HADDOCK	**	Similar in appearance to cod but smaller with dark patch near the gills on each side of the body

HAKE	**	Similar to cod and haddock but has a longer head— has soft white flesh with good flavour. The bones are larger and more easily detached than with most fish

HALIBUT	***	The largest flat fish available in Britain. It has firm white flesh. Usually sold cut into slices. Very expensive

HERRING	**	The herring has the greatest nutritional value of all British fish. They are relatively small fish with a lot of fine bones. There are concentric rings on the scales which indicate the age of the fish. Avoid fish with bloodshot eyes

HUSS (Flake, Rigg, Dogfish)	*	Firm meaty fish always sold skinned

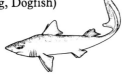

JOHN DORY	**	Has a high narrow body and is highly esteemed by gastronomes. Flesh firm and white and rather similar to cod

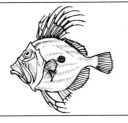

STARS REFER AS FOLLOWS: *Relatively cheap fish **Medium priced fish ***Expensive fish
(In cases where fish is available in both fresh and processed forms, star rating refers to price when sold fresh.)

SEASONAL AVAILABILITY	PROCESSED FORMS	PREPARATION OF FRESH FISH	COOKING
Available all year. Best: Oct-Jan	Smoked Hot smoked (smokies) Frozen	Whole or fillets	Suitable for all methods. Also for made dishes of all kinds. Good cold
Available all year. Best: Nov-Jun	–	Fillets, steaks or whole	Suitable for all methods. Also for made dishes of all kinds. Good cold
Available all year. Best: Jul-Mar	–	Steaks or cuts	Suitable for all methods. Also for made dishes of all kinds. Good cold
Available all year. Best: Jul-Nov. British-caught herring are scarce at present	Smoked (kipper, bloater, buckling) Salted Pickled Marinated Canned Frozen	Whole or filleted. Allow 1-2 per person. Salted herring: Soak in cold water for 12 hours, changing the water occasionally, then boil	Suitable for all methods of cooking. Good cold or soused
Plentiful all year. Best: Nov-Jul	–	Cuts	Deep fry or poach. Suitable for made dishes
Rare except some southern ports. Best: Jan-Apr	–	Fillets	Poach, steam, bake or grill

Note: The drawings in this chart are not to scale.

FISH		DESCRIPTION

LING 	★	Elongated cod-like fish
MACKEREL 	★	A nourishing fish with distinctive green and grey striped markings on its back. Usually about 30cm/12in long and weighing from 350g/12oz to 450g/1lb. Should be eaten very fresh. Avoid limp fish
MONKFISH (Angler Fish) 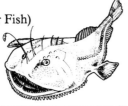	★★	This fish is a ray-like shark. All of the body behind the head to the tail usually appears on the fishmonger's slab ready skinned
MULLET: GREY 	★★	Steel-grey fish usually between 38-63cm/15-25in long
MULLET: RED 	★★★	Small red fish, grows up to 15cm/6in long. The flesh is firm and has a very good flavour
PERCH 		Most common of the British freshwater fish. The flesh is firm and white and with a good flavour. Difficult to obtain at the fishmonger's

STARS REFER AS FOLLOWS: *Relatively cheap fish   **Medium priced fish   ***Expensive fish
(In cases where fish is available in both fresh and processed forms, star rating refers to price when sold fresh.)

SEASONAL AVAILABILITY	PROCESSED FORMS	PREPARATION OF FRESH FISH	COOKING
More common on West Coast. Aug-Mar	Salted Dried	Steaks or fillets. Soak salted ling in cold water for 24 hours before using. Change the water from time to time	Fry or bake. Use in made dishes. Grill steaks
Plentiful, particularly on West Coast. Best: Nov-Feb and in Scotland in Aug	Smoked Canned Frozen	Whole or filleted	Suitable for all methods, also for some made dishes. When smoked, good in salads
Available all year	–	Steaks, wash well	Fry or bake. When deep fried it is similar to scampi
Particularly in the South. Jul-Feb	–	Whole	Bake or poach
Particularly in the South. Apr-Oct	–	Whole. The liver is considered to be a delicacy and should be left in the fish	Bake, fry or grill
Jun-Feb	–	Whole. Difficult to scale. Remove scales by plunging into boiling water for 1 minute, then remove with back of a knife. Be careful when handling fish as dorsal spikes dangerous	Poach, fry or bake

Note: The drawings in this chart are not to scale.

FISH		DESCRIPTION
PIKE		A river fish which grows to quite a large size. Difficult to obtain at the fishmonger's
PILCHARDS		* Large fish are usually sold whole. Small pilchards are sardines
PLAICE		** Plaice is a popular flat fish with yellow to reddish-brown spots on the dark side, the other side being white
POLLACK		* A white fish similar to coley
REDFISH		* Bright salmon-red fish with a spiny frill along the back. Should not be mistaken for the smaller red mullet which has a much better flavour
ROACH		Freshwater fish of not very good flavour and very bony. Rudd is a similar fish

STARS REFER AS FOLLOWS: *Relatively cheap fish **Medium priced fish ***Expensive fish
(In cases where fish is available in both fresh and processed forms, star rating refers to price when sold fresh.)

SEASONAL AVAILABILITY	PROCESSED FORMS	PREPARATION OF FRESH FISH	COOKING
Jul-Feb	–	Soak for 3-4 hours in salted water before using. Remove scales as for perch (see above)	Poach, fry or bake
Available only in southern waters. Sep-Mar	Canned	–	Grill
Plentiful all year. Best: Jun-Dec	–	Whole or filleted. A 1kg/2lb fish will give four 100g/4oz fillets	Suitable for all methods. Also good cold
Scarce. Best: Oct-Mar	–	Fillets or steaks	Suitable for all methods
Scarce. Best: Jul-Mar	–	Fillets	Poach, grill or bake
Sep-Mar	–	–	Use in soups

Note: The drawings in this chart are not to scale.

FISH		DESCRIPTION

SALMON  ★★★ The flesh has a delicate pink colour and excellent flavour

SALMON TROUT  ★★★ Same species as brown trout but which has spent part of its life in sea water. Similar in appearance to grilse

SARDINES  ★ These are young pilchards

SHAD  Large fish. Not often found on the fishmonger's slab

SKATE 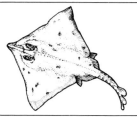 ★ Always sold in pieces called 'wings'

SMELTS (Sparling)  ★★ These are very small freshwater fish with a delicate flavour

STARS REFER AS FOLLOWS: *Relatively cheap fish **Medium priced fish ***Expensive fish
(In cases where fish is available in both fresh and processed forms, star rating refers to price when sold fresh.)

SEASONAL AVAILABILITY	PROCESSED FORMS	PREPARATION OF FRESH FISH	COOKING
Imported all year. English and Scottish: Feb-Aug; Irish: Jan-Sep	Smoked Canned Frozen	Whole or steaks	Poach, grill or bake. Excellent cold
Mar-Aug	–	Whole or steaks	Poach, grill or bake. Excellent cold
Available irregularly in the South	Canned	Whole	Grill or fry
West Coast	–	Whole or fillets	Poach; if red, grill or bake
Sep-Feb	–	Wings	Poach or fry
Scarce. Best: Oct-Apr	–	Whole	Fry or bake

Note: The drawings in this chart are not to scale.

FISH		DESCRIPTION

SOLE: DOVER		***	Much esteemed flat fish. The colour of the dark surface is a nearly uniform dark brown. The side of the head opposite the eyes is covered with numerous soft papillae
SOLE: LEMON		**	Similar to the Dover sole, but not in the same class. The dark side of the fish has a brown/yellow colour and is freckled with light brown spots
SPRATS		*	Sprats are very small fish resembling young herring. Their usual length is up to 10-13cm/4-5in and their colouring is similar to herring
TENCH			Freshwater fish taken from ponds and rivers. Similar to carp but smaller
TROUT		**	Freshwater fish with a profusion of red speckles on its side
TUNA		***	Rarely available fresh at the fishmonger. The flesh is pink like salmon

STARS REFER AS FOLLOWS: *Relatively cheap fish **Medium priced fish ***Expensive fish
(In cases where fish is available in both fresh and processed forms, star rating refers to price when sold fresh.)

SEASONAL AVAILABILITY	PROCESSED FORMS	PREPARATION OF FRESH FISH	COOKING
Plentiful all year. Best: Apr-Jan	Frozen	Whole or fillets, usually skinned before cooking	Suitable for all methods
Plentiful Apr-Dec	Frozen	Whole or fillets, usually skinned before cooking	Suitable for all methods
Plentiful Oct-Mar	Smoked	–	Fry or grill
–	–	Whole, stand in salted water for 2-3 hours and then scald in boiling water to remove scales	Bake, fry or grill. Use carp recipes
Farm-produced trout available all year. River-trout: Mar-Sep	Smoked Frozen	Whole	Suitable for all methods
–	Canned	Steaks or cuts	Grill. Canned tuna can be used for a variety of made dishes

Note: The drawings in this chart are not to scale.

FISH		DESCRIPTION

TURBOT 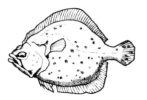 ★★★ A large flat fish with firm, white flesh
and a good flavour, usually sold cut into pieces

WHITEBAIT  ★★ Very small herring or sprat, silvery in colour

WHITING  ★ Small fish with a pale silver skin.
They are delicate and easily digested

SHELLFISH

COCKLES  ★ Small bivalve shellfish

CRAB  ★★ Crabs should be heavy in proportion to their size
and if sold cooked should be a bright reddish colour
with stiff joints. Hold by the claws and shake:
if it swishes with water, it is of inferior quality

STARS REFER AS FOLLOWS: *Relatively cheap fish **Medium priced fish ***Expensive fish
(In cases where fish is available in both fresh and processed forms, star rating refers to price when sold fresh.)

SEASONAL AVAILABILITY	PROCESSED FORMS	PREPARATION OF FRESH FISH	COOKING
Available all year. Best: Apr-Aug	–	Steaks or cuts	Steam, grill, bake or poach. Very good cold. Use halibut recipes
Feb-Jul	Frozen	Whole	Deep fry
Plentiful all year. Best: Dec-Feb	Smoked	Whole or filleted	Suitable for all methods and for made dishes
Available all year	Pickled	Prepare as directed in Chapter 2	Boil, steam or bake
May-Aug	Frozen Canned	Prepare as directed in Chapter 2	Boil and serve cold and dressed, or use in made dishes

Note: The drawings in this chart are not to scale.

FISH		DESCRIPTION

CRAYFISH		*** This is the name given to shellfish very akin to lobster. They have an average market length of 7.5-10cm/3-4in and are usually sold cooked

LOBSTER		*** Lobsters should be heavy in proportion to their size. The shell is blue-black when alive and bright red if sold cooked. If fresh the tail of the lobster will spring back sharply when pulled out straight. Usually sold cooked. Very expensive

MUSSELS		* Bivalve shellfish with blue-black shell which should be tightly closed and have a sharp edge

OYSTERS		*** Large bivalve shellfish which must be very, very fresh. The shells should be tightly closed

PERIWINKLES		* Small dark, round shellfish (similar to whelks but smaller)

PRAWNS		** Shellfish similar to crayfish. Usually sold cooked. They should be bright pink or red in colour

STARS REFER AS FOLLOWS: *Relatively cheap fish **Medium priced fish ***Expensive fish
(In cases where fish is available in both fresh and processed forms, star rating refers to price when sold fresh.)

SEASONAL AVAILABILITY	PROCESSED FORMS	PREPARATION OF FRESH FISH	COOKING
Available Sep-Apr	–	Prepare as directed in Chapter 2	Boil or fry or use in made dishes
Available all year. Best: in summer. Closed season Scotland: Jun-Aug	Canned	Prepare as directed in Chapter 2	Bake or grill, or boil and serve cold, or use in made dishes
Plentiful Jul-Aug. Best: Aug-Nov	Frozen Canned Pickled Smoked	Prepare as directed in Chapter 2	Boil, steam or bake. Use in made dishes
Native: Sep-Jun	Frozen Canned Smoked	Open the shell by inserting a knife at the hinge and snap the ligament which attaches the fish to the flat shell. Check freshness	Eat raw or boil, poach or shallow fry. Use in made dishes
Available all year. Best: Apr-Aug	–	Wash well and soak in salted water. Boil for 20 minutes. Remove flesh from shell by inserting a pin and twisting	See previous column
Plentiful all year. Best: Feb-Oct	Frozen Canned	Prepare as directed in Chapter 2	Grill or use in made dishes. Good cold

Note: The drawings in this chart are not to scale.

FISH			DESCRIPTION
SCALLOPS		★★★	A bivalve similar to oysters. The roe should be full and a bright orange colour. Usually sold cooked and with the shells open
QUEEN SCALLOPS		★★	Bivalves that deserve greater popularity, rarely seen at the fishmonger. Sometimes incorrectly referred to as clams
SCAMPI	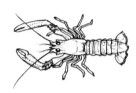	★★★	These are Norway lobster or Dublin Bay prawns. They are naturally pale orange-pink in colour and do not change colour on cooking
SHRIMPS		★★	Small prawns. Usually sold cooked. Avoid those with limp tails.
SQUID	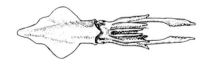	★	Popular in Italy as calamari. Squid is a mollusc
WHELKS		★	Small round shellfish

STARS REFER AS FOLLOWS: *Relatively cheap fish **Medium priced fish ***Expensive fish
(In cases where fish is available in both fresh and processed forms, star rating refers to price when sold fresh.)

SEASONAL AVAILABILITY	PROCESSED FORMS	PREPARATION OF FRESH FISH	COOKING
Plentiful Oct-Mar	Frozen	If opening at home, place on a warm stove and when they are open remove black part and any gritty fibre. Wash and use shell again	Poach, grill, bake, fry or use in made dishes
Available from West Coast of Ireland, Scotland, Wales and South West England. Oct-Mar	Frozen	Prepare as above	Cook as above
Available all year	Frozen	Prepare as directed in Chapter 2	Grill or use in made dishes. Good cold
Plentiful all year. Best: Feb-Oct	Frozen Canned Potted	Prepare as directed in Chapter 2	Fry or use in made dishes. Good cold
Available all year	–	Remove transparent central spine, viscera and mucous membrane from body pouch, pull off any outer skin. Cut tentacles away from head. Use body and tentacles. Wash well.	Boil, fry or use in made dishes. Good cold
Plentiful all year	–	Prepare as directed in Chapter 2	Boil or fry

Note: The drawings in this chart are not to scale.

C20 207 800x

FISH		DESCRIPTION

FISH ROES

CAVIAR	★★★	This is the salted roe of the sturgeon. It comes in various colours: black, yellow, grey, dark green and brown
COD ROE	★★	In all fish the hard roe is that of the female fish and the soft roe that of the male fish. Cod roe sold in the shops is usually hard
HERRING ROE	★★	Herring roe sold in the shops is usually soft
LUMPFISH	★★	This roe is similar to black caviar but much cheaper

STARS REFER AS FOLLOWS: *Relatively cheap fish **Medium priced fish ***Expensive fish
(In cases where fish is available in both fresh and processed forms, star rating refers to price when sold fresh.)

SEASONAL AVAILABILITY	PROCESSED FORMS	PREPARATION OF FRESH FISH	COOKING
Available all year	Canned In jars	–	Serve with lemon juice, and bread or toast
Available all year	Smoked Canned	–	Fry or use in made dishes
Available all year	Canned	–	Fry or use in made dishes
Available all year	Canned In jars	–	Serve with lemon juice, and bread or toast

2 Preparing and Preserving Fish

Most commercially caught fish is gutted at sea and the fishmonger will automatically cut up the larger fish to offer a choice of steaks and fillets. Those fish which are sold whole – such as mackerel, trout and herring – the fishmonger will scale, clean and cut into fillets on request. Shellfish – with the exception of bivalves like oysters and mussels – is usually sold ready cooked.

If, however, you have an angler in the family or you buy from the local market or live close to one of the fishing ports, it is a good idea to know how to tackle the job of preparing fish at home. Keep heads, skin and bone to make fish stock. (Indeed if you are buying from a fishmonger there is no reason why you shouldn't also request these items along with the filleted fish.) Here are a few guidelines to follow:

Scaling Fish

Some fish such as mullet and herring have thick, coarse scales which must be removed before cleaning the fish.
1 Place the fish on kitchen paper to catch the scales.
2 Cut off the fins with a sharp pair of scissors.
3 Take hold of the tail of the fish and scrape the fish all over with the back of a knife.
4 Wash well to remove loose scales.

Cleaning Fish

Clean all fish on a piece of kitchen paper or newspaper so that the entrails can be wrapped up and immediately thrown away.

Round fish:
1 Using a pair of kitchen scissors or a sharp knife, cut the belly of the fish, cutting from the gills lengthways towards the tail to a point about two thirds the length of the fish.
2 Remove all the entrails but retain the roe which has a good flavour and is high in food value.
3 Rinse thoroughly, making sure that any black tissue is removed, and pat dry.

4 If desired, remove the head by cutting across behind the gills. Trout are usually served with their heads intact, whereas mackerel often have their heads removed before cleaning which makes the process easier to accomplish.

Flat fish:
1 Place the fish dark skin up on kitchen paper.
2 Locate the gills and cut out.
3 Open up the belly which is just behind the head and the gills and clean out thoroughly.
4 Remove the head making a semi-circular cut at the base of the head. Dover sole usually retains its head for serving.
5 Trim the fins and tail back to the body with sharp scissors.

Skinning Fish

Removing the skin from the whole uncooked fish can be a little difficult. It is much easier to skin after the fish has been cooked. However, there are occasions when a skinned fish is required for the recipe. Dover sole, for example, should have at least the dark skin removed because it is extremely coarse. Great difficulty will be experienced in skinning fish that is not completely fresh. Round fish are not generally skinned before cooking.

Flat fish:
1 Lay fish on a wooden board, white side down and trim the fins and tail with sharp scissors.
2 Scrape the tail end of the fish with the back of a knife until the skin starts to lift.
3 Make a slit at this point and push the end of a round bladed knife under the skin. Carefully loosen the skin from the flesh working towards the head.
4 When enough skin has been loosened, the skin will pull off from tail to head.
5 Repeat this process on the white surface if required.

Fillets:
1 Place skin side down on a board.
2 Firmly hold the tail end of the fillet and with the aid of a knife, roll the flesh away from the skin, working from tail to head. Take care not to cut into the flesh.
Note: A little salt on the hand holding the fish helps to prevent slipping.

Filleting or Boning Fish

Filleting means removing the flesh from the head and bones in two or four pieces.

Round fish:
1 Lay the cleaned fish on its side on a board.
2 Insert a sharp knife under the small bones at the side of the cleaned belly cavity and prise up. Do this on both sides.
3 Next, insert the point of the knife into the back of the fish just behind the head and cut down the backbone to the tail.
4 Keeping the knife flat, slice the fillet free of the bones and then turn over and slice the second fillet free.
5 Remove any small bones still adhering to the fillet and wash.

Herring, mackerel and trout:
These round fish can be filleted as directed above or they can be boned to give one large double fillet.
1 Remove the head and with a sharp knife or kitchen scissors slit the belly of the fish down from the head end to the tail.
2 Remove entrails and roes. Rinse well and pat dry.
3 Open up the fish gently and place it on a board inside down.
4 Press hard along the full length of the backbone to loosen it.
5 Turn over and, starting at the head end, lift up the backbone and pull it steadily away from the flesh.
6 Cut off end of bone and the tail.
7 Rinse and check for any remaining bones.

Flat fish:
1 Lay the cleaned fish on a board with the tail towards you.
2 With a sharp knife slit the fish down the backbone.
3 Turn the knife so that it is flat against the bone and cut the flesh free to the edge.
4 Repeat the process with the second fillet and then turn over and cut out the other two fillets in the same way.

Preparing Skate
Only the 'wings' are used for cooking. These are cut from either side of the backbone.
1 Skate carries a good deal of natural slime and this should be scrubbed off.
2 Remove the dark skin by nicking out a small piece of flesh on the thick side of the wing to provide something to grip.
3 Using a strong pair of pliers, grip the skin at this point and pull it off in one piece.
4 Cut out the sharp hooks that may remain embedded in the flesh after skinning.

Dealing with Live Shellfish

Most shellfish are killed by being plunged into boiling salted water. However, crabs must be killed humanely before being boiled.

Lobster and crayfish:

Cooking lobster:
1 Wash well and tie the claws securely.
2 Plunge head first into plenty of fast boiling salted water.
3 Return to the boil quickly and then simmer for 20-30 minutes according to size. Take care not to cook for too long or the flesh will be tough.
4 Plunge into cold water for 2 minutes, drain and leave to cool. Alternatively the lobster can be cut in two lengthways and baked in the oven. It should first be killed by driving a sharp knife between the body and the tail, to sever the spinal cord.

Dressing lobster:
1 Twist off the claws and crack them with a hammer taking care not to crush or splinter them.
2 Split the lobster from head to tail.
3 Remove the meat, discarding the gills, the stomach sac in the head and the dark intestinal filament which runs down the tail.
4 Cut the meat into chunks and use to fill the cleaned cavity.
5 Serve on a bed of lettuce and arrange the claws around the head.

Cooking crayfish:
1 Wash well.
2 Plunge into plenty of fast boiling salted water.
3 Simmer for about 10 minutes.
4 Drain and leave to cool.

Shelling crayfish:
1 Separate the tail from the body.
2 Peel the shell from the tail.
3 Carefully remove the dark intestinal filament.

Prawns, shrimps and scampi:

Cooking prawns and shrimps:
1 Wash well. Place shrimps in a wire basket or tie up in muslin.
2 Plunge prawns or shrimps into fast boiling salted water.
3 Leave to cook for about 8 minutes. They are ready when they have changed colour.
4 Drain and leave to cool.

Shelling prawns and shrimps:
1 Hold the head of the prawn or shrimp firmly in the right hand and the tail in the left.

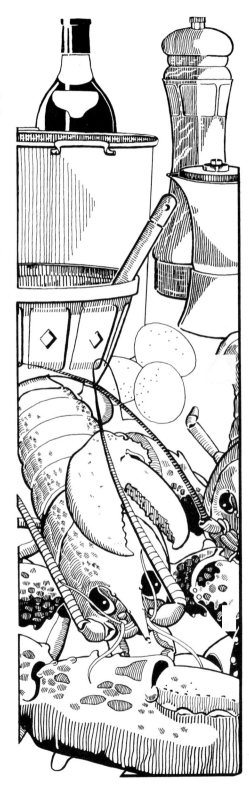

2 Straighten the body of the fish and with a twist of the right hand draw the shell off. It should come off almost whole. Fresh prawns shell much more easily than stale ones.

Cooking and shelling scampi:
Follow instructions for crayfish, above.

Crab:

Cooking crab:
1 Run an awl behind the eyes to kill.
2 Tie the claws together and plunge into boiling salted water.
3 Bring quickly back to the boil and simmer for 20-30 minutes according to the size of the crab.
4 Plunge crab into cold water, drain and leave to cool.

Dressing crab:
1 Turn the crab on its back and twist off the claws and the flap.
2 Insert the fingers between the body and the shell and force apart.
3 Remove all the inedible parts. These include the poisonous 'fingers' or gills which will be found stuck to the sides of the shell, the small stomach sac which is placed near to the head and the small greenish intestines.
4 Remove the crabmeat from the shell and keep on one side.
5 Wash and dry the shell.
6 Crack the claws with a hammer, taking care not to crush or splinter them, and remove the meat.
7 Mix all crabmeat with a little oil and vinegar dressing and some fresh breadcrumbs. Season to taste.
8 Fill the shell with this mixture and decorate with chopped egg, parsley and a few small claws.

Cockles, mussels and whelks:

Cooking cockles, mussels and whelks:
1 Thoroughly scrub the outside of the shells and remove all crustacea and any beard.
2 Stand for about 2 hours in cold salted water to clean.
3 Drain and leave to stand for a few minutes. Discard any bivalves that do not close fully.
4 Plunge into boiling salted water or cook according to the recipe.
5 Discard any bivalves that have not opened during cooking.
   If you have time, mussels can be cleansed and fattened by leaving overnight in a large bucket sprinkled with coarse oatmeal. Allow about 225g/8oz oatmeal to every 2.5 litres/4 pints mussels. Give the bucket a shake and place in a dark cupboard.

Next day, drain and proceed as usual, omitting the standing time in step 2.

Freezing Fish

Only the very freshest fish and shellfish should be frozen. *Never* freeze fish from the fishmonger; the delay in transporting the catch to the shop will affect both the flavour and the keeping qualities of the fish. This is particularly true of shellfish which must be freshly caught and cooked at once before freezing.

All fish should be gutted before freezing. Small fish such as trout and herring can be left whole but large fish should have their heads and tails removed. Alternatively the fish can be cut into fillets or steaks before freezing.

Wash white fish in salt water before drying and wrapping. Oily fish, however, should be washed in plain water as the combination of salt and fat would cause deterioration when the fish is in the freezer.

The choice of packaging is particularly important in freezing fish both to ensure that the fish is thoroughly protected from the air, and that it will not break through the wrappings, and also to prevent a fishy smell from being transferred to other items in the freezer. With this last point in mind take care to rinse your hands thoroughly after washing and preparing the fish before packaging it.

Always freeze fish in a freezer marked with the international freezing symbol. This is a large star together with 3 smaller stars, such as those found on a fridge. This shows that the machine is capable of freezing a stated quantity of food to −18°C/0°F or below within 24 hours. Never try to freeze fish in the icebox of a fridge.

There are a number of different methods of freezing fish. They include the following:

Dry pack: Prepare fish and wrap in freezer film or foil, making sure that there is a double layer of packaging between each fish or piece of fish. This makes for easy separation when the fish is required. Pack into polythene bags or rigid containers, excluding all air. This is very important for if air is left in the pack the fish will become dry and tasteless. Freeze quickly in the fast freeze section of the freezer.

Acid pack: Prepare a solution of citric acid powder, allowing about 1 teaspoon to 600ml/1pint water. Dip the prepared fish in this solution and then drain, wrap, seal and freeze as above. This is a useful method to use when freezing steaks and fillets of white fish as it helps to preserve the flavour and whiteness of the fish.

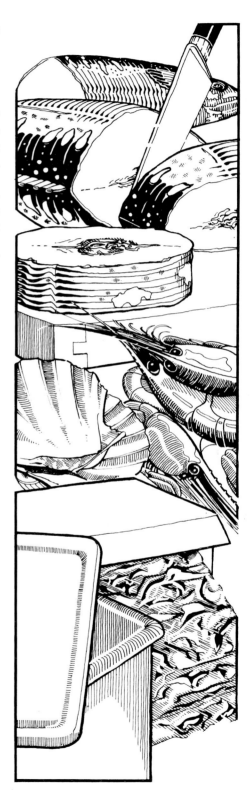

Brine pack: Prepare a solution of salt water, allowing about 1 tablespoon salt to 1.2 litres/2 pints water. Dip the prepared fish in this solution and then drain, wrap, seal and freeze as above. This pack is not suitable for oily fish as the mixture of fat and salt can cause rancidity.

Solid ice pack: Layer small fish fillets or steaks in a rigid container separating the layers with a double layer of freezer film or foil. Fill with water and freeze solid in the fast freeze section of the freezer. Remove the ice block from the container and wrap in freezer film or foil to store.

Open freezing:: Place the prepared fish uncovered in the very coldest part of the fast freezing section. When frozen solid, wrap in freezer film or foil and return to the freezer to store

Glazed whole fish: Open freeze cleaned unwrapped fish. When frozen solid, dip it quickly into very cold water so that a thin film of ice forms on the fish. Replace in the freezer for an hour and then repeat the water dipping process. Continue until the ice is about 5mm/¼in thick and then wrap in freezer film or foil.

Freezer Storage Life

Do not try to freeze too much fish at once as it should not be stored for too long in the freezer. Both flavour and texture are lost with long-term storage. Fish which has been salted and smoked will not keep as long as fresh fish. Guidelines to storage are as follows:

Type of fish	Maximum storage time
White fish	6 months
White fish (brine pack)	4 months
Oily fish	4 months
Smoked fish	3 months
Shellfish	1 month

Thin fillets of white fish and kippers may be cooked straight from the freezer but most fish will taste better if thawed first. Thaw in wrappings or container in the fridge. Allow about 5-6 hours per 450g/1lb.

Fish Freezing Chart

Type of fish:	Preparation	Packaging	Freezing method
White fish	Clean, wash and leave whole or cut into steaks or fillets	Polythene bags; rigid container	Dry pack; acid pack; brine pack; solid ice pack
	Coat fillets with breadcrumbs	Polythene; foil	Open freeze and pack
Oily fish	Clean, wash and leave whole or cut into steaks or fillets	Polythene bags; rigid container	Dry pack; solid ice pack; open freeze and glaze
Smoked fish	Wash and dry	Polythene bags; foil	Dry pack
Lobster and crayfish	Cook	Polythene bags; rigid container	Dry pack
Prawns, shrimps and scampi	Cook, cool and shell	Polythene bags; rigid container	Dry pack; open freeze and pack; open freeze and glaze
	For potted shrimps, cover shrimps with melted spiced butter, and cool	Rigid container	Dry pack
Scallops	Open shells and remove fish. Wash in salt water and pack in fresh salt water: 1 teaspoon salt to 600ml/1pint water leaving 2.5cm/1in headspace	Rigid container	Brine pack (solid)
Mussels	Cook. Remove from shell and pack, covering with juices	Rigid container	Wet pack
Crab	Cook. Clean crab and remove edible meat. Scrub shell and retain	Rigid container with polythene bag for shell	Dry pack

Salting Fish

Salting is a very old method of preservation which relies on the action of salt to inhibit the growth of bacteria, yeast and moulds and stop the action of enzymes occurring naturally in the food. Fish can be dry salted by layering with salt in a barrel or earthenware container, or it can be immersed in a solution of brine (450g/1lb salt to 2.5 litres / 4 pints cold water). Very often fish is brined before being dry salted as this draws out the blood and other fluids. Only common, kitchen, cooking or block salt should be used for salting, though sea salt can be used for brining. Table salt should not be used as it has chemicals added to ensure that it flows freely and these can affect the salting process.

Once again only the freshest fish should be used and all containers and utensils should be scrupulously clean. Temperature control is also very important and fish should be processed in the fridge. Nothing metallic should be used.

Herrings are the most generally salted fish in Britain but salt cod is popular in some countries. In Scandinavia salmon is also lightly salted and eaten raw.

The fish must not come into contact with the air and must be kept under the brine all the time.

It is sensible to check the brine bath once a week and if it has become sticky or discoloured it should be drained off and the food washed, wiped and put back in fresh brine in a clean container. (If you are using a dry salting recipe, you will at this point need to make up a brine solution.)

Salted Herrings

1kg/2lb herring fillets
225g/8oz common salt
12 black peppercorns
3 bay leaves

Arrange the salt and fish in layers in a cooled earthenware container starting and ending with salt, and sprinkling peppercorns and bay leaves as you go. Cover and weigh down. Place in the fridge. After a few days check that the salt has drawn out the liquid from the fish and formed a brine. Check the brine at weekly intervals, and leave the fish in the brine for 3-4 weeks before eating.

The salted herrings can be kept in the fridge for up to 6 months. As many as are required may be taken from the brine and soaked in water for a few hours before use.

Scandinavian Salted Salmon
(Gravlaks)

Leave the skin on the fish and pat dry with a clean cloth. Mix together all the ingredients except the dill and rub all over the fish halves. Place half the dill in a shallow earthenware dish and lay a piece of salmon skin side down on top. Spread the remainder of the dill over the salmon and place the second piece of salmon on top, skin side up. Cover with foil or greaseproof paper and place heavy weights on top. Keep in the fridge for 3 days.

To serve, remove excess salt and peppercorns from the fish and slice on the slant into pieces slightly thicker than those used for smoked salmon.

450g/1lb salmon, head removed, split in half and boned
25g/1oz castor sugar
25g/1oz common salt
8 white peppercorns
1 teaspoon ground coriander
1 tablespoon dried dill, soaked in water, or 1 bunch fresh dill

Smoking Fish

Smoking fish at home is not really practicable unless you have a large garden and a good source of really fresh fish. Fish can be hot smoked which is not really a method of preserving as much as a tasty way of cooking it, or cold smoked. In the latter process the fish is not cooked and should be lightly brined first.

Hot smoking:

You will need a smoke box, available from specialist camping stores. Cover the base of the smoke box with a thin layer of sawdust, taking care not to use too much. Add the drip tray and the inverted basket and place the fish on top. Herring, mackerel, trout and any freshly caught raw fish can be used. Close the lid and mount the smoke box on the heat source. Adjust the heat so that the sawdust gently smoulders. Halfway through the cooking time the fish should be turned over and the lid replaced. Allow about 8 minutes each side for herring and 10-15 minutes for trout and mackerel, depending on their size.

Hot smoked fish must be eaten at once or within two or three days if stored in the fridge.

Cold smoking:

Cold smokers can be bought commercially or they can be improvised from an old oil drum. All the seams will need to be sealed and two holes cut — one in the side and one in the top. The difference between a cold smoker and a hot one is that the smoke is generated outside the smoker for cold smoking and fed into the smoker through a pipe let into the hole at the side. A chimney is fixed to the hole at the top to allow the smoke to escape after circulating round the fish.

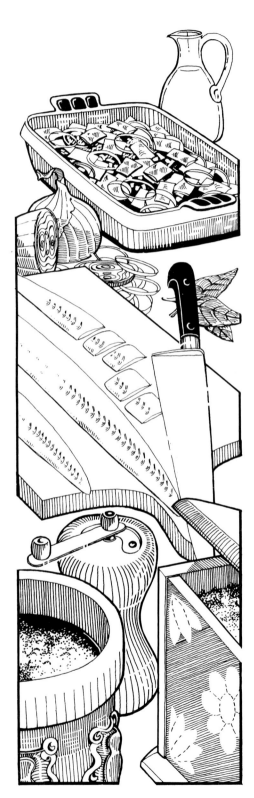

The temperature in the cold smoker is much lower than in a hot smoker and the fish is not cooked. The ideal temperature for fish is about 21°C/70°F and a thermometer will be needed to keep a check on the temperature.

The heat source for keeping the sawdust smouldering is housed in the base of the fire box which should be a nearly closed grate. A pipe is used to carry the smoke from the fire box to the smoker. This pipe must be at least 30cm/12in long to allow the smoke to cool before entering the smoker. Aromatic woods such as juniper or bay may be used with sawdust to give a special flavour. Avoid the use of resinous woods such as pine.

Suitable fish for cold smoking include whiting, herring, haddock, plaice, trout, mackerel, salmon and eel.

Fish for cold smoking must first be brined for 3-4 hours in a solution of 450g/1lb salt to 2.5 litres/4 pints cold water. After this time drain, wash and dry. Next dry salt allowing 850g/1¾lb salt to each 2.5kg/5lb of fish. Stand for a further 2-3 hours and then rinse well. Hang to dry in a cool airy place. An electric fan set on cold is helpful. The fish is ready to smoke after 1-3 hours depending on weight. It should look smooth and shiny.

Place the fish in the cold smoker and hang clear of the sides and each other. To some extent the length of time of smoking depends on personal taste, but here are some general guidelines:

Type of fish	Time
Herring, whiting	6-8 hours
Plaice	8 hours
Haddock	12 hours
Trout, mackerel	12-14 hours
Eel	24 hours
Salmon	Up to 4 days, depending on size

Fish must be smoked continuously so a long, slow burning fire is essential.

Smoked fish should be air dried and then wrapped and stored in the fridge. It can be kept for up to 3 months. Freezing is not recommended for home smoked fish.

Pickling Fish

Fish may be pickled at home but it will not keep as long as commercially pickled fish. The fish must be really fresh and the vinegar must have an acetic acid content of at least 5 per cent. Most branded vinegars are suitable for pickling.

Herrings are the fish most usually pickled. They should be scaled and cleaned and then soaked in vinegar overnight. The next day fillet the fish and arrange the layers in an earthenware dish. Sprinkle each layer with salt and pepper and some sliced raw onion. Add a bay leaf or two along the way.

Place in the fridge and leave to stand for 24 hours. The herrings may now be eaten or again covered in vinegar and used as desired over the next week.

A Scottish method of pickling herrings is slightly different. The fish is filleted and cut into strips about 1cm/½in wide. These are layered in a dish with sliced onion, salt, pepper and 3 tablespoons brown sugar. Cover with vinegar and eat the next day or any time during the following week.

Rollmop herrings are made by first brining the herring fillets in a mixture of 225g/8oz salt to 1.2litres/2pints water for 24 hours. Drain off the brine and replace with a fresh solution. After a further 24 hours rinse the herring fillets thoroughly in cold water. Roll each fillet up with a little sliced onion in the centre and skewer with a cocktail stick. Pack into jars with some peppercorns and cover with vinegar which has been steeped with pickling spices. Screw on the tops of the jars, making sure that they are vinegar proof, and keep for up to 8 weeks in a cool place.

3 Basic Cooking Methods

The most important rule to bear in mind when cooking fish or shellfish is that they should be cooked for as short a time as possible. Overcooking results in hard, dry and tasteless fish. To test whether the fish is cooked or not, press gently at the thickest part. If fully cooked the fish will flake easily and leave the bone. Fillets are cooked when a creamy white substance begins to run from the fish. Add shellfish to made up dishes at the last minute for this has already been cooked once.

Poaching

Large fish are best poached in a fish kettle which has a metal rack for lifting in and out of the kettle. However, any pan that is the right size can be used and the fish lowered in and out on a sling of muslin. Avoid using more liquor than that required just to cover the fish.

The liquor may vary according to the recipe but will usually be made up of one of the following: wine, wine and water, cider, milk and water or a *court-bouillon* which is a specially prepared stock for fish.

Step-by-Step Guide to Poaching
1 Prepare the poaching liquor and bring to just below boiling.
2 Place prepared fish in the pan, bring to the boil and reduce the heat to allow the liquor to simmer.
3 Test to see if the fish is cooked and remove from the pan.
4 Drain thoroughly and serve with one of the sauces or garnishes given in Chapter 4.

Type of fish	Time
Whole thin fish or very large steaks	10 minutes
Whole fat fish or very large steaks	15 minutes
Small fillets	5 minutes
Small steaks	6 minutes

Whole fish or large steaks can also be placed in cold poaching liquor and brought to the boil. The fish is then boiled rapidly for a very short time and left to stand in the cooking liquor. Salmon is particularly good cooked in this manner. Unless the fish is very large, boil for 1 minute and leave to stand in the cooking liquor for 15 minutes if the fish is to be served hot or it can be left until cold.

General Court-Bouillon

1.2 litres/2 pints water
1 tablespoon cider or wine
   vinegar
1 onion, sliced
1 carrot, sliced
2 sprigs thyme
2 teaspoons chopped parsley
2 teaspoons salt
4 peppercorns

White Court-Bouillon for Turbot and Halibut

600ml/1pint white wine or
   cider
600ml/1pint water
150ml/¼pint milk
2 teaspoons salt
2 slices lemon

Basic Fish Stock

Place all the ingredients in a large pan. Bring to the boil, cover and simmer for 1 hour. Strain and use in sauces and other made dishes. For a stronger stock, return the liquid to the pan after straining and reduce over a high heat.

750ml/1¼pints water
1-2 fish heads
bones and skin from filleted
   fish
1 onion, chopped
1 carrot, chopped
1 bay leaf

Steaming

This method of cooking fish is most suitable for small fillets or thin steaks and is the best way to cook fish for invalids.
1 Place the fish on a well-greased soup plate. Sprinkle with salt and pepper and dot with a little butter.
2 Place the soup plate on a pan of boiling water or cooking vegetables and cover with the saucepan lid or an inverted plate.

3 Steam for 10-15 minutes and test to see if it is cooked.

4 Serve with the fish liquor poured over it.

Large cuts and whole fish can also be steamed but will need to be cooked in a steamer.

1 Butter the base of the steaming rack or wrap the fish in buttered greaseproof paper.

2 Steam over simmering water until cooked. Allow the same time as for poaching. Do not allow the water to go off the boil.

3 Test at the thickest part and serve with one of the sauces or garnishes given in Chapter 4.

Grilling

Grilling is suitable for steaks or fillets and for small whole fish such as plaice, dab, sole or herring. White fish can be wrapped in well-oiled greaseproof paper and grilled in this.

1 Preheat the grill and grease the grid to help prevent the fish sticking to it.

2 Cut small whole round fish across in deep gashes to allow the heat to penetrate, otherwise the outside of the fish will dry up before the inside is cooked.

3 Season the fish and brush white fish with a little oil or melted butter. Baste again during grilling. Oily fish do not need any extra fat for grilling.

4 Place the fish under the grill and cook fillets until tender. Steaks and whole fish will need to be turned over halfway through the cooking time. Use a fish slice and turn the fish very carefully to avoid breaking it up.

5 The time taken to grill fish varies from 5-20 minutes, depending on size and thickness. Fillets of plaice for example will be ready within 5 minutes, whereas a trout or mackerel may need up to 10 minutes each side.

Shallow Frying

Fillets and thin steaks or small whole fish are the most suitable fish for shallow frying. Large fish or thick steaks cannot be cooked successfully by this method.

Fish for shallow frying must first be thoroughly dried, seasoned and then coated with flour. Shake off any excess flour as this will only burn in the pan. Alternatively, small fillets can be dipped in milk or beaten egg and then in flour or fine breadcrumbs. Herrings are sometimes coated in fine oatmeal.

1 Season fish and dip in chosen coating.

2 Melt fat in the pan and heat until it is fairly hot. For thin fillets, heat enough fat to cover the bottom of the pan; for thicker fillets or steaks and small whole fish, heat enough fat to come a little way up the fish.

3 Fry the coated fish until golden brown and then carefully turn over and brown the other side.
4 Thin fillets will be cooked at this stage but thicker fish may need to have the heat lowered after it is nicely browned and the cooking continued until tender. Allow 5-6 minutes in total for thin fillets, 8-10 minutes for thicker fillets and 12-14 minutes for steaks and whole fish.

Dry Frying

Herrings, pilchards, sprats and sardines can be dry fried in a very thick frying pan. Sprinkle the pan with salt and heat it, shaking occasionally, until very hot. Place the fish in the pan and fry until golden and crisp on both sides.

Deep Frying

Deep frying is an excellent method of cooking fillets and steaks, very small whole fish such as whitebait, and fish cakes and croquettes. The fish must be thoroughly dried, seasoned and coated with flour, egg and breadcrumbs or batter.

Thin Flour Batter with Breadcrumbs

Mix the flour and seasoning together and add the water gradually to mix to the consistency of thin cream. Dip the fish in the batter and then in breadcrumbs.

50g/2oz flour
salt, pepper
150ml/¼ pint water
breadcrumbs

Thick Batter

Mix together the flour and seasoning. Add the beaten egg and just enough milk or water to mix to a stiff batter that will coat the back of a spoon thickly. Dip the fish in flour and shake off any excess and then dip in the batter making sure that it is evenly coated.

100g/4oz flour
salt, pepper
1 egg, beaten
about 5 tablespoons milk or
    water

1 Use a deep heavy pan and pour in sufficient fat to cover the fish but not to come more than halfway up the pan. This is important because some of the surface moisture on the food will boil violently in the fat and could cause it to boil over if the pan is too shallow.
2 Heat the fat gently with the basket in the fat. When it stops bubbling and a faint blue haze starts to rise it is hot enough to use. Do not allow the fat to smoke or it will spoil the fish. The temperature of the fat may be tested by dropping in a 2.5cm/1in cube of stale bread. If the fat is hot enough the

bread will brown in 1 minute and the temperature will be approximately 190°C/375°F. If a sugar or fat thermometer is available the following are the correct temperatures to use. (Heat the thermometer with the fat and do not allow it to touch the base of the pan.)

Type of fish	Temperature	Approximate cooking time
Croquettes and cakes	180°C/350°F	3-4 minutes
Scallops and scampi	182°C/360°F	3 minutes
Whitebait	190°C/375°F	4-5 minutes
Fillets of fish	190°C/375°F	4-6 minutes
Fried potatoes	199°C/390°F	5-8 minutes

3 Drop the coated fish into the hot fat and cook as indicated above. Do not try to fry too much fish at once as this reduces the temperature of the fat and the fish will be pale and greasy instead of well browned and crisp.
4 As soon as the fish is cooked, drain on absorbent paper and serve hot.
5 Strain the fat through a very fine sieve or muslin and use again.

Oven Frying

This method is suitable for fillets and steaks.
1 Season the fish and then coat with one of the following: egg and browned breadcrumbs; milk and browned breadcrumbs; milk and oatmeal.
2 Heat 25g/1oz cooking fat in an ovenproof dish and place the fish in this.
3 Cover with a piece of greased paper and bake at 220°C/425°F/Mark 7 for 30 minutes. Serve with a sauce from Chapter 4.

Baking

All cuts and types of fish may be baked in the oven either in covered casseroles or in earthenware dishes with a covering of foil or greaseproof paper. Whole fish may be stuffed or fillets rolled round fillings of various kinds. The fish may be sprinkled with a topping of cheese and breadcrumbs or baked with tomatoes and onions. The variations are endless. A number of different recipes for baking fish are given in Chapters 6 and 8.

Baking in a Fish Brick

Some shops sell porous earthenware fish bricks. They are used as follows:

1 Line the base with buttered greaseproof paper to make it easier to clean.
2 Place the cleaned and seasoned fish in the brick together with any stuffing or flavourings. Use fresh herbs, shallots, capers, mustard or tomatoes.
3 Cover with the top of the brick and place in a *cold* oven.
4 Raise the heat to 230°C/450°F/Mark 8 and cook for 25-30 minutes.
5 After use wash out the brick but do not use detergents or the smell may linger in the brick.

Serving Fish

Whole large fish are usually placed on the table on the bone and then served off the bone. Using a fish knife and fork work along the backbone of the fish lifting blocks of flesh off one side and then the other. When the whole of the backbone is revealed this is removed and the lower side of the fish served. Small whole fish may be served as they are or boned.

To bone cooked round fish such as herring:
1 Slit down the centre of the back from head to tail, inserting the knife just far enough to touch the backbone.
2 Lay back the flesh on the uppermost side thus revealing the backbone with the smaller bones attached to it.
3 Insert the knife under the backbone and lift the bone out gently. It should come away clean.

To bone small flat fish such as sole:
1 Cut off the head and ease off the bony frill on each side of the fish.
2 Slit down the centre of the back from head to tail, inserting the knife just far enough to touch the backbone.
3 Ease up the fillet free of the bone on one side working from tail to head and lay at an angle to the body. Repeat the process with the second fillet.
4 Cut across the tail and ease out the backbone.
5 Replace the top fillets over the bottom ones and serve.

4 Sauces and Garnishes

Sauces and garnishes are an essential part of fish cookery. Whether the fish is an expensive one or not, it will benefit enormously by the addition of a delicious sauce. However, there is no need to drown the fish and quite small quantities of the richer sauces will be sufficient.

The flavour of the sauce depends to a large extent on the richness of the liquid base. If, for example, the recipe calls for fish stock it is possible simply to use the liquor the fish was cooked in. However, if the bones and head are added to the liquor and this is then reduced by rapid boiling the resultant stock will be much stronger and will give a better flavour to the sauce.

There are a number of basic sauces such as Velouté — made with butter, flour and stock, Béchamel — made with butter, flour and flavoured milk or milk and stock, and Espagnole — made with browned butter and flour and a good brown stock. Recipes for these sauces are given later in this chapter and many of the other sauces use these as a base.

The thickness of the sauce will depend upon the ratio of butter and flour to liquid. A very thin masking sauce uses 25g/1oz each butter and flour to 600ml/1pint liquid; a medium sauce uses about 40-50g/1½-2oz each; and a thick binding mix about 75-100g/3-4oz each.

Other sauces use eggs rather than flour as their thickening agent and these include Hollandaise and Béarnaise, among others. Cold sauces are usually, though not always, egg based.

Fish which is cooked with a rich butter-based sauce is often flashed under a hot grill to obtain a thin golden coating on the surface of the sauce. The grill must be very hot as this glazing process must be a rapid one or the rich sauces will curdle.

Light and complete gratins are two other processes for finishing off certain fish dishes. A light gratin is carried out half-way through the cooking process and consists of sprinkling the fish with fine brown breadcrumbs and dashing it with melted butter. The dish is then returned to a hot oven, to finish cooking and to brown lightly.

In a complete gratin the fish is coated with sauce, sprinkled with a mixture of two thirds grated cheese and one third white breadcrumbs, dashed with melted butter and browned quickly in a hot oven, or under a pre-heated grill.

Both fish and fish sauces tend to have little colour of their own and clever garnishing can help to make a dish look more attractive. Choose a selection from the garnishes set out at the end of this chapter.

Hot Sauces

Béchamel Sauce

Put milk or milk and stock in a saucepan with the onion, mace, bay leaf, bouquet garni and peppercorns and bring to the boil. Turn off the heat and leave to stand for 30 minutes and then strain. Melt the butter in a pan and stir in the flour. Stir and cook for a few seconds. Add the strained liquid gradually, stirring all the time. Bring the mixture to the boil and simmer for 5 minutes. Add salt, nutmeg and cayenne to taste.

600ml/1pint milk or milk and
  fish stock
1 small onion
1 blade mace
1 bay leaf
1 bouquet garni
3 peppercorns
50g/2oz butter
50g/2oz flour
salt, nutmeg, cayenne

Espagnole Sauce

Fry the streaky bacon in the oil. Add the carrot, onion and celery and fry for 5 minutes. Add the tomatoes to the mixture with the parsley. Dissolve the stock cube in the water and pour into the pan. Bring to the boil and cook until the liquid has reduced by one third. Strain and set on one side. Melt the butter in a saucepan and let it brown slightly. Add the flour and stir in. Cook until it becomes nicely browned. Gradually add the prepared stock, stirring all the time. Bring to the boil and simmer gently for 15 minutes. Season to taste and add sherry if desired.

50g/2oz streaky bacon, diced
1 tablespoon oil
1 carrot, chopped
1 onion, chopped
1 stick celery, trimmed and
  chopped
3 tomatoes, chopped
1 tablespoon chopped parsley
1 beef stock cube
900ml/1½pints water
50g/2oz butter
50g/2oz flour
salt, pepper
1 tablespoon sherry (optional)

Velouté Sauce

50g/2oz butter
50g/2oz flour
600ml/1pint strong fish stock
salt, pepper

Melt the butter in a pan, add the flour. Stir and cook for a few seconds, taking care not to brown the mixture. Gradually add the fish stock, stirring all the time. Continue stirring until the mixture thickens. Season and continue cooking gently for 5 minutes.

Ale and Anchovy Sauce

300ml/½pint thick béchamel
  sauce (**page 59**)
150ml/¼pint light ale
1 onion, coarsely chopped
2 teaspoons anchovy essence
salt, pepper
2 tablespoons double cream

Make a thick béchamel sauce using 40g/1½oz each butter and flour to 300ml/½pint flavoured milk. Pour the light ale into a pan, add the onion and bring to the boil. Simmer for 5 minutes, strain and add the liquor to the thick béchamel sauce. Stir and bring to the boil. Add anchovy essence and season to taste. Remove from the heat and add cream.

Anchovy Sauce

300ml/½pint thick béchamel
  sauce (**page 59**)
150ml/¼pint double cream
1 tablespoon anchovy essence
salt, pepper

Make a thick béchamel sauce using 40g/1½oz each butter and flour to 300ml/½pint flavoured milk. Add cream and anchovy essence and correct seasoning. Heat through but do not boil.

Béarnaise Sauce

150ml/¼pint dry white wine
150ml/¼pint tarragon vinegar
1 shallot, chopped
175g/6oz unsalted butter
4 egg yolks
1 teaspoon chopped parsley
  (optional)
1 teaspoon chopped tarragon
  (optional)
salt, pepper

Place the wine and vinegar in a pan with the shallot. Boil rapidly until reduced by half. Strain into a basin and leave to cool. Add half the butter to the cooled mixture and place the basin over a pan of barely simmering water. Stir until the butter has melted. Whisk one egg yolk at a time into the vinegar and butter mixture. Continue whisking until the mixture thickens. Whisk in the rest of the butter in small pieces. Add herbs and seasoning to taste. Do not allow the mixture to boil.

Beetroot Sauce

Melt butter in a pan and cook the onion and garlic until soft. Add the flour and stir well. Cook until lightly browned. Place beetroot with vinegar in a blender, blend until smooth and stir into the sauce. Bring to the boil, stirring all the time. Remove from the heat, season and add cream.

50g/2oz butter
1 onion, finely chopped
1 clove garlic, chopped
15g/½oz flour
2 small beetroot, cooked,
    peeled and roughly chopped
150ml/¼pint vinegar
salt, pepper
2 tablespoons single cream

Bordelaise Sauce

Simmer the onion in red wine with herbs for 10 minutes. Add fish stock and bring to the boil. Whisk in butter and lemon juice and season to taste. Remove the bay leaf and serve with grilled whole fish.

1 small onion, finely minced
150ml/¼pint red wine
1 tablespoon chopped parsley
¼ teaspoon dried thyme
1 bay leaf
150ml/¼pint strong fish stock
50g/2oz butter
2 tablespoons lemon juice
salt, pepper

Breton Sauce

Fry the mushrooms and garlic in the oil for 5 minutes. Mix with tomato purée. Make the espagnole sauce and stir in the tomato and mushroom mixture and simmer for 2 minutes. Add parsley and serve at once.

50g/2oz mushrooms, finely
    minced
1 clove garlic, minced
1 tablespoon oil
2 tablespoons tomato purée
600ml/1 pint espagnole sauce
    (page 59)
1 teaspoon chopped parsley

Butter Sauce

This is a sauce made with melted clarified butter which is mixed with one of the following: anchovy essence; chopped tarragon; chopped hard-boiled eggs; vinegar.

Caper Sauce

400ml/¾pint cream sauce (**see below**)
2 tablespoons lemon juice
3 tablespoons capers

Make the cream sauce and just before serving add lemon juice and capers. Heat through but do not allow to boil.

Cheese Sauce

600ml/1pint béchamel sauce (**page 59**)
100g/4oz grated cheese
1-2 tablespoons single cream

Make the béchamel sauce and then stir in the grated cheese. Cheese tends to thicken the sauce so use a little single cream to give the required consistency.

Clarified Butter

Place the desired amount of butter in a small pan and let it melt slowly over a low heat. Skim off all the scum that rises as the butter heats. When no more scum appears pour the butter off very carefully, keeping back the sediment. The butter is now clarified and ready to use.

Cream Sauce

300ml/½pint thick béchamel sauce (**page 59**)
150ml/¼pint double cream
salt, pepper

Make a thick béchamel sauce using 40g/1½oz each butter and flour to 300ml/½pint flavoured milk. Add the cream and seasoning and heat through. Do not allow to boil.

Creole Sauce

50g/2oz butter
1 onion, finely chopped
1 small green pepper, deseeded and finely chopped
¼ teaspoon dried mixed herbs
400g/14oz canned tomatoes
salt, pepper, garlic salt, paprika

Melt butter in a pan. Fry the onion and pepper for 5 minutes. Add remaining ingredients and bring to the boil. Simmer for 15-20 minutes, stirring occasionally to break up the tomatoes. Serve as it is or for a smoother effect blend for a few seconds and reheat.

Egg and Lemon Sauce

Beat egg yolks in a basin and then add the lemon juice and fish stock. Whisk until the mixture is really light and frothy. Place over a pan of barely simmering water and continue whisking until the mixture thickens. Serve with fried or poached fish.

4 egg yolks
juice 2 lemons
4 tablespoons fish stock

Gooseberry Sauce

Poach the gooseberries in a little water until tender. Blend or rub through a sieve and return the purée to the pan. Add sugar and butter and heat till boiling.

225g/8oz gooseberries, topped and tailed
50g/2oz sugar
50g/2oz butter

Greek Sauce

Make the velouté sauce. Add the olives to it with the lemon juice.

600ml/1pint velouté sauce **(page 60)**
75g/3oz stuffed olives, finely chopped
juice ½ lemon

Hollandaise Sauce

Boil the vinegar until reduced by half. Leave to cool. Whisk the egg yolks and cooled vinegar in a basin set over a pan of barely simmering water, until the mixture begins to thicken. Then gradually whisk in the butter until all is absorbed. Season and add lemon juice to taste. Serve at once.

2 tablespoons wine vinegar
3 egg yolks
100g/4oz unsalted butter, cut into small pieces
salt, pepper
juice ½ lemon

Lemon Sauce

Mix the cornflour with the lemon juice until smooth. Heat the stock and gradually add the mixed cornflour, stirring all the time. Bring to the boil and simmer for 3-4 minutes. Remove from the heat. Beat the eggs together in a basin, pour in the sauce and stir. Return to the pan and bring slowly to the boil, stirring all the time. Season to taste and serve.

15g/½oz cornflour
juice 2 lemons
400ml/¾pint fish stock
2 eggs
salt, pepper

Mousseline Sauce

150ml/¼pint double cream
4 egg yolks
pepper
25g/1oz butter, melted
1 teaspoon lemon juice

Place the cream, egg yolks and pepper in a basin set over a pan of barely simmering water. Whisk as the mixture heats and thickens. Add the butter a little at a time, making sure that each addition is well incorporated before adding the next. The finished sauce should resemble frothy cream. Just before serving add the lemon juice.

Mushroom Sauce

175g/6oz button mushrooms, finely chopped
2 tablespoons cooking oil
2 tablespoons flour
about 250ml/8floz milk
salt, pepper

Fry the mushrooms gently in the oil for 5 minutes. Add flour and stir well. Gradually add the milk, stirring all the time. Bring the mixture to the boil and cook for 5-8 minutes. Add more liquid if the sauce gets too thick. Season to taste.

Oyster Sauce

400ml/¾pint béchamel sauce **(page 59)**
12 oysters, opened and removed from shells
25g/1oz butter
1 teaspoon lemon juice
salt, pepper
1 tablespoon double cream

Make the béchamel sauce. Place the oysters in a small saucepan with their own liquor and the butter. Cover and simmer very gently for 5 minutes but do not allow them to boil. Remove the oysters from the pan and cut into quarters. Reduce the oyster liquor to half its original quantity and strain. Return to the saucepan, add the béchamel sauce, oysters and lemon juice. Heat through and season to taste. Remove from the heat, add cream and serve.

Parsley Sauce

600ml/1pint béchamel sauce **(page 59)**
3-4 tablespoons finely chopped parsley

Make a béchamel sauce and just before serving add the parsley.

Peanut Sauce

100g/4oz peanut butter
150ml/¼pint milk
juice 1 lemon
salt, black pepper
fish stock

Place the peanut butter in a pan and gradually blend with the milk. Add the lemon juice, pepper and salt if desired, and bring to the boil. If the mixture is too thick add a little lfishs stock to give the required consistency. Serve with white fish.
Note: If unsalted peanut butter is used, salt will need to be added to taste.

Piquant Sauce

Make the espagnole sauce. Add the onion, gherkins and capers to it with the parsley and vinegar. Bring to the boil, simmer for 10 minutes and season to taste.

300ml/½pint espagnole sauce **(page 59)**
1 onion, finely chopped
3 gherkins, finely chopped
2 tablespoons capers, finely chopped
2 tablespoons chopped parsley
1 tablespoon vinegar
salt, pepper

Ravigote Sauce

Make the cream sauce and add the herbs and vinegar. Heat through, without boiling, and serve.

400ml/¾pint cream sauce **(page 62)**
2 teaspoons chopped chives
2 teaspoons chopped parsley
2 teaspoons chopped chervil
2 teaspoons chopped tarragon
1 tablespoon white wine vinegar

Red Wine Sauce

Place carrots and mushrooms in a pan with the red wine and bring to the boil. Boil until the liquid has reduced by half. Make the espagnole sauce and add the wine and vegetables. Add the ham to the sauce and season to taste.

25g/1oz carrots, cut into matchsticks
25g/1oz mushrooms, thinly sliced
300ml/½pint red wine
300ml/½pint espagnole sauce **(page 59)**
25g/1oz ham, cut into thin strips
salt, pepper

Sauce Bercy

Sauté the shallots in half the butter. Do not allow to brown. Melt remaining butter in a pan and add flour. Stir and add the fish stock and wine, stirring all the time. Bring to the boil and simmer for 5 minutes. Add shallots and parsley and season to taste.

12 shallots, sliced
40g/1½oz butter
25g/1oz flour
300ml/½pint fish stock
150ml/¼pint white wine
6 tablespoons chopped parsley
salt, pepper

Tomato Sauce

450g/1lb tomatoes, coarsely
    chopped
2 tablespoons tomato purée
150ml/¼pint water
salt, pepper
pinch dried marjoram

Place all the ingredients in a pan. Bring to the boil and cook for 15 minutes. Place in a blender and blend until smooth. Reheat and serve.

Watercress Sauce

300ml/½pint velouté sauce
    (page 60)
2 bunches watercress, washed
    and picked over
50g/2oz butter
salt, pepper, cayenne
lemon juice

Make the velouté sauce. Boil the watercress in salted water until tender. Drain and mince. Add the butter and mix well. Bring the velouté sauce to the boil and remove from the heat. Add the watercress and butter mixture a little at a time, beating well between each addition. Season to taste with salt, pepper, cayenne and a dash of lemon juice. Serve at once.

White Wine Sauce

300ml/½pint white wine
600ml/1pint stock
1 bay leaf
2 black peppercorns
1 clove
1 small onion, chopped
50g/2oz butter
50g/2oz flour
salt, pepper

Place wine, stock, bay leaf, peppercorns, clove and onion in a pan and bring to the boil. Continue cooking until the liquid has reduced by one third. Strain and set on one side. Melt butter in a pan and add flour. Stir and cook for a few seconds. Gradually add the prepared stock, stirring all the time. Bring to the boil, season and continue cooking for 5 minutes.

Cold Sauces

Mayonnaise

2 egg yolks
salt, pepper
½ teaspoon French mustard
300ml/½pint olive oil
2 teaspoons wine vinegar

Beat together the egg yolks, seasoning and mustard. Continue beating with a whisk while the oil is added a few drops at a time. As the oil is gradually used up it may be poured in a little faster but do not try to hurry the process. Finally, add the vinegar.

Chaud-Froid

Make up the aspic jelly as directed on the packet and, when cool, mix with mayonnaise. Use to coat cold poached or steamed fish.

150ml/¼pint aspic jelly
300ml/½pint mayonnaise (**page 66**)

Elizabethan Sauce

Place breadcrumbs in a basin and mix with lemon juice, wine vinegar, spices and seasoning and leave to stand for 1 hour. Remove clove and mace and blend to give a smooth texture. Fold into mayonnaise. Thin with a little cream if the mixture is too thick.

50g/2oz dark rye breadcrumbs
3 tablespoons lemon juice
1 tablespoon wine vinegar
¼ teaspoon ground cinnamon
1 clove
1 blade mace
salt, pepper
150ml/¼pint mayonnaise (**page 66**)
single cream (optional)

Horseradish Sauce

Whip cream stiffly and fold in remaining ingredients.
Note: 300ml/½pint cream may be used, without mayonnaise. Flavour with a little prepared mustard.

150ml/¼pint double cream
150ml/¼pint mayonnaise (**page 66**)
75g/3oz horseradish root, grated

Rémoulade Sauce

Mix all ingredients carefully together.

300ml/½pint mayonnaise (**page 66**)
1 teaspoon chopped tarragon
1 teaspoon chopped parsley
1 teaspoon chopped chervil
1 teaspoon chopped gherkins
1 teaspoon chopped capers
1 teaspoon chopped chives
1 teaspoon French mustard (optional)

Tartar Sauce

2 teaspoons finely chopped
   shallots or spring onions
15g/½oz gherkins, finely
   chopped
15g/½oz olives or capers, finely
   chopped
1 teaspoon chopped parsley
300ml/½pint mayonnaise (**page
   66**)
tarragon vinegar (optional)

Stir the shallots, gherkins, olives and parsley into the mayonnaise. Thin with a little tarragon vinegar if necessary.

Country Sauce

3 hard-boiled eggs, separated
4 tablespoons olive oil
300ml/½pint soured cream
1 tablespoon chopped chives
salt
sugar
3 tablespoons white wine

Rub the egg yolks through a sieve and blend with the olive oil. Add cream, chives, and salt and sugar to taste. Finely chop the egg whites and add to the sauce. Gradually stir in the wine and mix well.

Vinaigrette

150ml/¼pint olive oil
3 tablespoons wine vinegar
1 teaspoon French mustard
salt, pepper
chopped parsley, chives or basil
   (optional)

Place all ingredients in a screw-top jar. Screw on the lid and shake very well.

Butters

Plainly grilled, fried, steamed or poached fish may be served garnished with little rounds of delicately-flavoured butter instead of sauce. Allow about 2-3 rounds for each piece of fish.

Anchovy Butter

Rinse the anchovies in cold water and rub through a sieve. Cream the butter and blend with the anchovies or essence. Blanch the parsley in boiling water and chop very finely. Add to the anchovy butter and blend well. Spread 5mm/¼in thick on a piece of greaseproof paper. Place in the fridge to set. When it is quite hard cut into fancy shapes or rounds with a pastry cutter.

6 anchovy fillets or 3 tablespoons anchovy essence
100g/4oz butter
1 sprig parsley

Herb Butter

Cream the butter and gradually add the lemon juice and herbs. Season to taste. Spread 5mm/¼in thick on a piece of greaseproof paper. Place in the fridge to set. When it is quite hard cut into fancy shapes or rounds with a pastry cutter.
Note: Any individual or mixture of fresh herbs can be used to make herb butters.

100g/4oz butter
juice ½ lemon
2 teaspoons chopped parsley
1 teaspoon chopped tarragon
1 teaspoon chopped chervil
salt, pepper

Horseradish Butter

Pound the horseradish in a bowl with the butter until really smooth and creamy. Season to taste. Spread 5mm/¼in thick on a piece of greaseproof paper. Place in the fridge to set. When it is really hard cut into fancy shapes or rounds with a pastry cutter.

4 tablespoons grated horseradish root
100g/4oz butter
salt, pepper

Mustard Butter

Cream the butter and gradually add the mustard, making sure that no lumps of dry powder remain in the mixture. Season to taste and spread 5mm/¼in thick on a piece of greaseproof paper. Place in the fridge to set. When it is really hard cut into fancy shapes or rounds with a pastry cutter.

100g/4oz butter
1 tablespoon dry mustard
salt, pepper

Paprika Butter

Sauté the shallots in a little of the butter with paprika. When the shallots are soft, rub through a sieve and cream with remaining butter. Add seasoning to taste. When the mixture is really smooth spread 5mm/¼in thick on a piece of greaseproof paper. Place in the fridge to set. When it is quite hard cut into fancy shapes or rounds with a pastry cutter.

4 shallots, finely chopped
100g/4oz butter
2 teaspoons paprika
salt, pepper

Parsley Butter

100g/4oz butter
juice ½ lemon
1 tablespoon chopped parsley
salt, pepper

Cream the butter and gradually add the lemon juice and parsley. Season to taste. Spread 5mm/¼in thick on a piece of greaseproof paper. Place in the fridge to set. When it is quite hard cut into fancy shapes or rounds with a pastry cutter.

Shrimp Butter

50g/2oz peeled shrimps or
  prawns
100g/4oz butter
black pepper

Rub the shrimps through a sieve. Cream the butter and mix with the shrimps. When the mixture is really smooth add black pepper to taste and spread 5mm/¼in thick on a piece of greaseproof paper. Place in the fridge to set. When it is quite hard cut into fancy shapes or rounds with a pastry cutter.

Soft Roe Butter

75g/3oz canned soft roes, or
  fresh, poached
75g/3oz butter
salt, pepper
½ teaspoon French mustard
  (optional)

Rub the roes through a sieve. Cream the butter and mix with the roes. Add seasoning and mustard if desired. When the mixture is really smooth spread 5mm/¼in thick on a piece of greaseproof paper. Place in the fridge to set. When it is quite hard cut into fancy shapes or rounds with a pastry cutter.

Tomato Butter

100g/4oz butter
2 tablespoons tomato purée
salt, pepper

Cream the butter and gradually add the tomato purée. Season to taste. When the mixture is really smooth spread 5mm/¼in thick on a piece of greaseproof paper. Place in the fridge to set. When it is really hard cut into fancy shapes or rounds with a pastry cutter.

Garnishes

Many fish dishes have a tendency to look rather colourless so brighten them up by using one or more of the following garnishes.

Fleurons

Roll out the pastry to about 5mm/¼in thick and cut into rounds or crescents with a pastry cutter. Place the cut-out pastry shapes on a greased baking tray and brush with beaten egg. Bake at 220°C/425°F/Mark 7 for about 8-10 minutes until golden brown and crisp.

100g/4oz puff or flaky pastry
1 egg, beaten

Cheese Fleurons

Roll out the puff pastry and sprinkle half the cheese over it. Fold in four and roll out again. Sprinkle with remaining cheese. Fold up and roll out once more and then cut into rounds or crescents with a pastry cutter. Place the cut-out shapes on a greased baking tray and bake at 220°C/425°F/Mark 7 for about 8-10 minutes until golden brown and crisp.

100g/4oz puff pastry
2 tablespoons grated Parmesan
cheese

Spiced or Herb Fleurons

Roll out the puff pastry and sprinkle half the spices or herbs over it. Fold in four and roll out again. Sprinkle with remaining spices or herbs. Fold up and roll out once more and then cut into rounds or crescents with a pastry cutter. Place the cut-out shapes on a greased baking tray and brush with beaten egg. Bake at 220°C/425°F/Mark 7 for about 8-10 minutes until golden brown and crisp.

100g/4oz puff pastry
1 teaspoon curry powder,
celery salt or dried mixed
herbs
1 egg, beaten

Artichoke Cups

Heat the artichoke bases in a pan in their own juice. Drain and place 1 tablespoon of the cheese sauce in each one. Sprinkle with breadcrumbs and brown under the grill.

400g/14oz canned artichoke
bases
150ml/¼pint cheese sauce
(page 62)
4 tablespoons breadcrumbs

Glazed Onions and Asparagus

Boil the onions in lightly salted water. As soon as the onions are tender, drain well and toss in melted butter with salt and pepper to taste. Drain the asparagus tips and heat through with a little butter. Arrange mounds of asparagus around the dish and alternate with glazed onions.

225g/8oz baby onions
25g/1oz butter, melted
salt, pepper
300g/10oz canned asparagus
tips

Lemon Twists and Butterflies

1 lemon, thinly sliced

For twists: cut each lemon slice halfway across and then twist the halves in opposite directions.

For butterflies: cut out a V-shape on either side of each slice. A piece of parsley may be placed in the centre if desired.

Mushroom Heads

8 large, flat mushrooms
butter
4 tablespoons breadcrumbs
50g/2oz smooth liver pâté
salt, pepper

Remove stalks from the mushrooms and dot with butter. Grill for about 3-4 minutes. Mix breadcrumbs with pâté and season to taste. Spoon the pâté mixture on to the grilled mushrooms, smooth over and dot with more butter. Replace under the grill for a further 3-4 minutes.

Olivette Potatoes

350g/12oz potatoes, cut into
  small rounds
25g/1oz butter
salt

Place the potatoes in a pan of cold water, bring to the boil and drain. Melt the butter in a pan and toss potatoes in this. Place in a casserole dish and bake at 200°C/400°F/Mark 6 until the potatoes are golden brown. Season with salt.

Potato Border

450g/1lb potatoes
1 egg yolk
15g/½oz butter
salt, pepper

Boil or steam the potatoes until tender. Sieve them and mix in the egg yolk and butter. Beat well over a very low heat and season to taste. When smooth and creamy put into a forcing bag and pipe a round or oval fluted border. This can be served at once or brushed with a little beaten egg and browned under the grill.

Stuffed Tomatoes

75g/3oz peeled prawns
150ml/¼pint thick béchamel
  sauce (**page 59**)
4 tomatoes, halved
salt, pepper

Make a thick béchamel sauce using 25g/1oz each butter and flour to 150ml/¼pint flavoured milk. Add the prawns and heat through. Grill the tomatoes, scoop out the centres, season and fill with prawn sauce. Replace under the grill to brown lightly.

5 Soups and Starters

Soups

Normandy Fish Soup

Sauté the onions in butter. Add the apple and the whiting. Pour on the cider and water and add the bay leaf, celery seed and pepper. Bring to the boil and simmer for 30 minutes. Put in a blender until smooth, or through a sieve, and then reheat. Remove from the heat. Mix the egg yolk and cream and pour into the soup. Stir 2 or 3 times and serve at once.

2 onions, sliced
15g/½oz butter
1 large cooking apple, cored and chopped
450g/1lb whiting, skinned, boned and cut into chunks
300ml/½pint cider
400ml/¾pint water
1 bay leaf
¼ teaspoon celery seed or celery salt
black pepper
1 egg yolk
4 tablespoons double cream

Cream of Coley Soup

Fry the onion in the oil until transparent. Add the sherry and bring to the boil. Add the fish to the onion mixture with the potatoes. Sprinkle over the herbs and pour in the milk and stock or water. Season and bring to the boil. Simmer for 45 minutes. Liquidise or rub through a sieve. Mix with cream and correct the seasoning. Reheat but do not allow to boil.

1 large onion, sliced
1 tablespoon oil
3 tablespoons medium sherry
350g/12oz coley, filleted and cut into chunks
350g/12oz potatoes, sliced
1 teaspoon dried chives
½ teaspoon dried dill
pinch dried marjoram
300ml/½pint milk
400ml/¾pint fish stock or water
salt, pepper
80ml/3floz double cream

Consommé Carmelite

1.2litres/2pints strong fish stock
2 tablespoons rice
1 tablespoon chopped dulse
   seaweed
salt, pepper

Place all ingredients together in a large saucepan and bring to the boil. Remove any scum and simmer for 15-20 minutes. Correct seasoning and serve with chunks of brown or black bread.

Portuguese Fish Soup

2 onions, finely chopped
1 clove garlic chopped,
   (optional)
2 tablespoons oil
450g/1lb canned tomatoes
juice 1 lemon
2 tablespoons chopped parsley
1 teaspoon dried mixed herbs
50g/2oz vermicelli
600ml/1pint fish stock or water
salt, pepper
8 fresh sardines, cleaned
4 slices French bread

Sauté the onions and garlic if used in oil until soft. Add the tomatoes, lemon juice, herbs, vermicelli, stock and seasoning. Bring to the boil and simmer for 15 minutes. Add the sardines and continue to simmer gently for 8-10 minutes until the fish are cooked through. Meanwhile toast the bread, searing it slightly. When the sardines are cooked, remove from the soup and keep hot to serve as the next course or leave to cool and serve with salad the following day. Place a round of well-toasted bread in each soup bowl and spoon the soup over the top. Serve at once.

Flounder and Spinach Soup

450g/1lb spinach, washed and
   picked over
1 bunch watercress, washed
   and picked over
750ml/1¼pints water or fish
   stock
1 clove garlic, crushed
salt, pepper
100g/4oz smoked mackerel
   fillet, skinned
450g/1lb flounders, cleaned and
   heads removed
2 large slices bread
oil for frying

Remove any tough stalks from the spinach and watercress. Place in a pan with the water or fish stock and bring to the boil. Add the garlic to the pan with salt and pepper. Add the mackerel fillet to the soup with the flounders. Simmer for 20-25 minutes. Take the flounders out of the soup and remove all skin and bones. Place the flesh in a blender with the rest of the soup and blend until thick and smooth. Fry the bread in the oil, drain and leave to cool. Cut into small squares. Reheat the soup and serve with the fried bread croûtons.

Cream of Herring and Oatmeal Soup

Sauté the onion in the oil until translucent. Add the oats and stir well. Next add the herrings, water or fish stock, bay leaves and seasoning and bring to the boil. Simmer for 30 minutes. Remove the fish from the liquor and remove the tails, backbones and any other large bones. Place the flesh in the blender with the rest of the soup and blend until thick and smooth. Make sure that the bones have been blended. Add the cream and reheat. Do not allow to boil.

1 large onion, finely sliced
2 tablespoons oil
2 tablespoons oatmeal or rolled oats
2 herrings, cleaned and heads removed
600ml/1pint water or fish stock
2 bay leaves
salt, pepper
150ml/¼pint single cream

Herring and Tomato Soup

Sauté the onions in butter until soft. Add the mushrooms with tomatoes, water or water and wine, vinegar and seasoning. Bring to the boil. Add the herring chunks to the soup. Simmer for 10 minutes and serve hot or cold.

2 onions, finely sliced
25g/1oz butter
100g/4oz button mushrooms, sliced
450g/1lb canned tomatoes
150ml/¼pint water or water and wine
1 tablespoon vinegar
salt, pepper
4 herrings, filleted and cut into chunks

Chilled Haddock Soup

Sauté the onion in oil for 3-4 minutes. Season and cover with fish stock and bring to the boil. Lay the fish on top of the onions and continue to simmer for 30 minutes. Remove fish, and skin and bone it. Mix the flesh with the onions and stock and liquidise in a blender. Leave to cool. Add double cream and milk and adjust the seasoning. Chill and serve garnished with parsley and egg yolk.

2 onions, sliced
2 tablespoons oil
salt, pepper
300ml/½pint fish stock
1 smoked haddock (about 600g/1¼lb)
300ml/½pint double cream
150ml/¼pint milk
1 tablespoon chopped parsley
1 hard-boiled egg yolk, sieved

New England Fish Chowder

100g/4oz streaky bacon, diced
2 tablespoons oil
2 large onions, sliced
600g/1¼lb potatoes, diced
400ml/¾pint milk
200ml/6floz water
1 teaspoon dried marjoram
salt, pepper
450g/1lb white fish fillets (cod, haddock, coley or huss), skinned and cut into chunks
100g/4oz peeled prawns

Fry the bacon in the oil. Add the onions to the pan and brown slightly. Add the potatoes with milk, water, marjoram and seasoning. Bring to the boil and simmer for 10 minutes. Add the fish and bring back to the boil. Continue simmering for a further 8-10 minutes until the fish is cooked. Add the prawns and serve in large bowls with French bread.
Note: This is a filling dish — so serve small quantities if using as a starter. It makes an excellent main course.

Mediterranean Fish Soup

2 large onions, coarsely chopped
2 tablespoons oil
1 clove garlic, crushed
1 small mackerel, cleaned
225g/8oz coley
225g/8oz whiting, cod or hake
450g/1lb fresh or canned tomatoes
2 tablespoons chopped parsley
½ teaspoon cayenne
1 bay leaf
grated rind ½lemon
salt, pepper, powdered saffron
1.2litres/2pints stock or water
150ml/¼pint white wine

This is an anglicised version of the fish soup popular all along the coast of Provence, using fish easily available in Britain.

Sauté the onions in the oil with the garlic. Add all other ingredients except the saffron and bring to the boil. Simmer for 30 minutes. Take out the fish and remove the head, skin and bones and return the flesh to the soup. Liquidise all the soup in a blender and add saffron to achieve the characteristic golden colour. Reheat and serve.
Note: This soup can provide the basis of an English version of *bouillabaisse,* the French fish stew. When you have made the soup simply poach mussels, prawns, red mullet and chunks of cod or hake in it for 10-15 minutes.

Cream of Shrimp Soup

25g/1oz butter
25g/1oz flour
750ml/1¼pints strong fish stock
1 egg yolk
1 tablespoon double cream
salt, pepper
75g/3oz peeled shrimps

Melt the butter in a pan and stir in the flour. Gradually add the fish stock, stirring all the time. Bring the mixture to the boil and simmer for 5 minutes. Remove from the heat and allow to cool a little. Mix egg yolk and cream and stir into the soup to thicken. Reheat but do not allow the mixture to boil. Season to taste and add shrimps. Serve at once.

Shrimp Bisque

Soak the breadcrumbs in a little of the fish stock and leave to stand for 5-10 minutes. Sauté the shrimps gently in the butter and add soaked breadcrumbs, remaining stock, lemon juice and seasonings. Bring to the boil and simmer for 5 minutes. Place in a blender and blend until really smooth. Stir in the cream and return to the pan. Reheat but do not boil.

50g/2oz breadcrumbs
750ml/1¼pints fish stock
350g/12oz peeled shrimps or
   prawns
25g/1oz butter
juice 1 lemon
salt, pepper, nutmeg
150ml/¼pint single cream

Corn and Crab Chowder

Fry the bacon in the oil. Add the onion and cook gently until translucent. Add the potatoes to the pan with the milk, water, basil and seasoning. Bring to the boil and simmer for 15 minutes. Add the sweetcorn and crabmeat and bring back to the boil. Simmer for 5 minutes. Adjust seasoning and serve.

100g/4oz streaky bacon, diced
1 tablespoon oil
1 large onion, sliced
600g/1¼lb potatoes, diced
400ml/¾pint milk
200ml/6floz water
½ teaspoon dried basil
salt, pepper
200g/7oz canned sweetcorn
225g/8oz white crabmeat

Salmon and Leek Soup

Sauté the onion and leeks in the oil. Add the potatoes, cook for 3-5 minutes and add the stock. Remove the bones and skin from the salmon. Flake the fish into the soup and add the dill. Season to taste. Bring to the boil and simmer for 10-15 minutes until the vegetables are tender.

1 large onion, coarsely chopped
4 medium leeks, trimmed and
   coarsely chopped
2 tablespoons oil
2 potatoes, diced
750ml/1¼pints vegetable or
   fish stock
200g/7oz canned salmon,
   drained
1 teaspoon chopped dill
salt, pepper

Chilled Scallop and Watercress Soup

4 scallops
2 bay leaves
150ml/¼ pint milk
1 large onion, sliced
1 tablespoon oil
3 tablespoons sherry
2 bunches watercress, washed
   and picked over
1 large potato, chopped
400ml/¾ pint stock
salt, pepper
1-2 teaspoons cornflour
4 tablespoons double cream

Poach the scallops with bay leaves in the milk for 5 minutes and set on one side. Sauté the onion gently in the oil until translucent. Add sherry and bring to the boil. Add watercress, potato, stock, the milk from the scallops and seasoning. Bring to the boil again and simmer for 40 minutes. Put in a blender; blend until smooth and return to the pan. Thicken with a little cornflour mixed with a little of the soup and bring to the boil. Remove from the heat and leave to cool. Place in the fridge to chill for 2 hours. Chop the scallops and add to the soup with the cream.

Starters

Spaghetti Salerno

175g/6oz spaghetti
75g/3oz butter
75g/3oz breadcrumbs
50g/2oz canned anchovy fillets,
   drained and chopped
350g/12oz broccoli, broken into
   florets
salt, pepper

Cook the spaghetti in lightly salted boiling water until just tender. Toss in 25g/1oz butter and keep warm. Fry the breadcrumbs in the remaining butter and add the anchovies. Cook the broccoli in boiling salted water until tender. Drain well, chop coarsely and season to taste. Place a portion of pasta on each plate and sprinkle on the breadcrumb and anchovy mixture. Top with broccoli and serve at once.

Pilchard Pâté

225g/8oz canned pilchards in
   tomato sauce
175g/6oz cream cheese
2 tablespoons lemon juice
garlic salt, paprika
2 tomatoes, sliced
1 tablespoon chopped parsley

Remove the pilchards from the sauce and mash well with a fork. Add cream cheese and beat well until really smooth. Add lemon juice and garlic salt and paprika to taste. If a stronger tasting pâté is preferred add a little of the sauce from the pilchards. Serve garnished with tomatoes and parsley, with fingers of hot toast.

Stuffed Onions

Steam the onions in a little salted water and allow to cool slightly. Remove the centres from the onions and chop finely. Mash the pilchards in their sauce and add the breadcrumbs, herbs and chopped onion centres. Season to taste and spoon the mixture into the centres of the cooked onions. Place the onions on a heat-proof plate and dot with butter. Bake at 200°C/400°F/Mark 6 for 15 minutes.

4 large or 8 small onions
150g/5oz canned pilchards in
    tomato sauce
25g/1oz breadcrumbs
1 teaspoon dried mixed herbs
salt, pepper
butter

Cucumber Madras

Drain mackerel and turn into a bowl. Mash well with a fork and mix in rice, raisins, mayonnaise and curry powder. Season to taste. Peel the cucumber first if you wish. Then cut it into 2 equal lengths, cut each piece in half lengthways and scoop out and discard the centre seeds. Fill the centre of the cucumber pieces with the mackerel mixture and serve on a bed of lettuce.

200g/7oz canned mackerel in
    oil
3 tablespoons cooked rice
1 tablespoon raisins
1 tablespoon mayonnaise
    (**page 66**)
1½-2 teaspoons curry powder
salt, pepper
½ large or 1 small cucumber
lettuce leaves

Smoked Mackerel Pâté

Melt the butter in a saucepan. Place mackerel, melted butter and lemon juice in a blender and blend until smooth. Add the cream cheese in small quantities and blend again. Season to taste and spoon into individual ramekin dishes. Place in the fridge to chill. Serve garnished with a little chopped parsley and very thin slices of lemon, with fingers of brown toast.

100g/4oz butter
350g/12oz smoked mackerel
    fillets, skinned
juice ½ lemon
75g/3oz cream or curd cheese
salt, pepper
chopped parsley
lemon slices

Smoked Mackerel Ramekins

Mash the mackerel fillets with a fork. Melt the butter in a pan and add the flour. Stir well and gradually add the milk, stirring all the time. When the sauce thickens, cook for 1 minute more and then remove from the heat. Add cheese and seasonings. Add the egg yolks to the sauce and then mix in the mashed mackerel fillets. Whisk the egg whites until they are really stiff and fold into the mackerel mixture. Quickly spoon into individual ramekin dishes and bake on a tray at 220°C/425°F/Mark 7 for about 12-15 minutes until well risen and golden brown. Serve at once.

225g/8oz smoked mackerel
    fillets, skinned
25g/1oz butter
15g/½oz flour
150ml/¼pint milk
25g/1oz grated cheese
salt, pepper
2 eggs, separated

Smoked Fish Mousse

1 smoked mackerel (350g/12oz),
  skinned and boned
225g/8oz canned tomatoes
25g/1oz gelatine
1 tablespoon lemon juice
1 tablespoon water
80ml/3floz double cream
3 eggs, separated
½ teaspoon dried marjoram
salt, pepper

Mash the mackerel with a fork. Place in a blender with the contents of the can of tomatoes and blend until smooth. Mix the gelatine in a cup with lemon juice and water and stand in a pan of hot water to dissolve. Whip cream until fairly thick and fold into the tomato fish mixture. Add gelatine, egg yolks and marjoram and season well. Whisk the egg whites until really stiff and fold into the fish mixture. Spoon into a mould and place in the fridge to set. Turn out and serve with hot tomato sauce (**page 66**) and brown bread and butter.

Moules Marinière

2.5litres/4pints mussels, well
  scrubbed
4 shallots, finely chopped
25g/1oz butter
½ teaspoon dried thyme
1 bay leaf, chopped
300ml/½pint dry white wine
black pepper
2 tablespoons chopped parsley

Make sure mussels are thoroughly clean. Remove limpets and beards and discard any mussels which are open. Place the shallots in a deep pan with butter, thyme and bay leaf. Gently fry for about 3-4 minutes and then add the mussels. Stir well. After a short while the mussels will open. Discard any that do not open. Add wine and black pepper and bring to the boil. Simmer for 10-15 minutes. Sprinkle with chopped parsley just before serving.

Baked Mussels

2.5litres/4pints mussels, well
  scrubbed
1 onion, chopped
600ml/1pint water
300ml/½pint dry white wine
2 sprigs parsley
½ teaspoon fennel seed
salt, pepper

Stuffing
75g/3oz breadcrumbs
½ teaspoon grated lemon rind
salt, pepper
25g/1oz grated Parmesan
  cheese
1 small onion, grated
1 clove garlic crushed (optional)
3 tablespoons chopped parsley

Make sure mussels are thoroughly clean. Remove limpets and beards and discard any mussels which are open. Place onion in a pan with the water, wine, parsley, fennel seed and seasoning. Add the mussels and bring to the boil. Fast boil for 2 minutes and then remove from the heat. Strain the liquor and keep on one side. Discard any mussels which have not opened. Pull the empty halves from the shells and arrange the filled halves on a well-buttered heat-resistant dish, packing them in closely.

To make the stuffing, mix the breadcrumbs with the lemon rind and seasoning and sprinkle over the mussels. Next, sprinkle with cheese and finally with the onion, garlic if used, and parsley. Boil up the cooking liquor from the mussels and reduce by half. Pour over the top of the mussels and cover loosely with kitchen foil. Bake at 190°C/375°F/Mark 5 for 20 minutes.

Smoky Corn Vol-au-vents (page 86)

Fried Squid

Dredge the squid in seasoned flour. Melt the butter with the oil in a frying pan and when the fat is hot add the squid. Fry for about 3 minutes, stirring the fish as it cooks. Be careful not to overcook or the flesh will go hard and rubbery. Serve with lemon wedges.

450g/1lb squid, cleaned and cut into rings
4 tablespoons seasoned flour
25g/1oz butter
2 tablespoons cooking oil
lemon wedges

Squid Salad

Plunge the squid into boiling water. Simmer for 5 minutes then drain and leave to cool. Mix the onion with the cold squid. Mix salad oil, vinegar, sugar and seasonings and pour over the fish. Sprinkle with chopped parsley, and serve with lemon wedges.

450g/1lb squid, cleaned and cut into rings
1 small onion, finely sliced
5 tablespoons salad oil
2 tablespoons wine or cider vinegar
sugar
salt, pepper
1 tablespoon chopped parsley
lemon wedges

Salade Niçoise

Arrange the lettuce in 1 large or 4 small bowls and add the chicory, celery, tomatoes, cucumber, beetroot, radishes and olives. Arrange the eggs on top of the salad with anchovies, green pepper rings and tuna. Just before serving, mix the oil and vinegar and pour over the salad. Sprinkle with black pepper.

lettuce leaves
chicory leaves, broken into pieces
4 sticks celery, trimmed and sliced
4 tomatoes, quartered
7.5cm/3in length cucumber, sliced
2 beetroots, cooked, peeled and diced
8 small radishes, trimmed
12-16 black olives
3 hard-boiled eggs, quartered
4 anchovy fillets
1 green pepper, deseeded and cut into rings
200g/7oz canned tuna, drained and flaked
80ml/3floz olive oil
2 tablespoons vinegar
black pepper

Devilled Scallops (page 95)

Tuna and Walnut Pâté

75g/3oz butter, softened
200g/7oz canned tuna, drained
  and mashed
25g/1oz walnut halves
2-3 shallots, finely chopped
1 teaspoon Worcestershire
  sauce
salt, pepper

Add the butter to the tuna and mix well. Reserve 4 walnut halves for decoration and chop the remainder. Add the chopped walnuts, shallots and Worcestershire sauce to the tuna mixture. Season to taste. Press into individual ramekin dishes and chill. To serve, turn out and decorate with reserved walnuts.

Herring and Apple Pâté

2 large fresh herrings, skinned
  and filleted
50g/2oz butter, softened
1 large dessert apple, finely
  grated
salt, pepper

Remove as many bones from the herring fillets as possible. Mince the fish and mix with softened butter. Add the apple to the mixture with salt and pepper. Mix well and press into individual ramekin dishes. Place in the fridge to chill. Serve with fingers of brown toast.

Devilled Herrings

3 herrings, skinned, filleted and
  cut into thin diagonal strips
25g/1oz seasoned flour
oil for deep frying
cayenne
Worcestershire sauce
lemon wedges

Toss the herring strips in the seasoned flour. Heat the oil and deep fry the herring strips in small batches, keeping each batch warm until all are cooked. Sprinkle with cayenne and a little Worcestershire sauce and serve with lemon wedges and brown bread and butter.

Herrings Madras

2 large fresh herrings, skinned
  and filleted
4 tablespoons wine or cider
  vinegar
2 tablespoons mayonnaise
  (page 66)
2 teaspoons curry powder
1 small onion, finely sliced
1 carrot, finely sliced
2 bay leaves
salt, pepper
lettuce leaves
sprigs watercress

Remove as many of the bones from the herring fillets as possible and cut into small pieces. Mix vinegar, mayonnaise and curry powder and place the herring pieces in the mixture. Add the onion and carrot to the mixture with the bay leaves and seasoning. Leave to stand for 2 hours. Remove bay leaves. Serve on a bed of lettuce and garnish with watercress.

Creamed Kipper Pâté

Place the kipper fillets in a blender with the single cream and lemon juice and blend quickly together. Season with black pepper and pour into individual ramekin dishes. Place in the fridge to chill. Serve with melba toast.

450g/1lb cooked kipper fillets, skinned
150ml/¼pint single cream
juice ½ lemon
black pepper

Kipper Vol-au-vents

Poach kippers in milk for 8-10 minutes and thaw peas for 1 minute in boiling water. Reserve the milk and skin and bone the kippers. Drain the peas. Make a thick sauce by melting the butter in a pan and adding the flour. Next add the milk from the kippers, stirring all the time. When the sauce thickens add the cheese, flaked kippers and peas. Continue cooking for 2-3 minutes. Pile into warmed vol-au-vent cases. Sprinkle with black pepper. Serve garnished with parsley.

225g/8oz kippers or 100g/4oz kipper fillets
150-200ml/6-7floz milk
50g/2oz frozen peas
15g/½oz butter
1 tablespoon flour
25g/1oz grated cheese
8 medium, baked vol-au-vent cases
black pepper
chopped parsley

Kipper Soufflé

Cook the kipper fillets as directed on the packet. Drain, retaining the liquid, flake and remove any bones. Melt the butter in a saucepan and add the flour. Stir well and add the milk and the liquid from the kipper fillets. Bring to the boil, stirring all the time. Remove from the heat and add the egg yolks to the sauce. Add the flaked kippers and season to taste. Whisk the egg whites very stiffly and fold into the kipper mixture. Grease a soufflé dish and pour the mixture into it. Bake at 200°C/400°F/Mark 6 for 30-35 minutes.

175g/6oz kipper fillets with butter
50g/2oz butter
50g/2oz flour
400ml/¾pint milk
4 eggs, separated
salt, pepper

Taramasalata

Soak the bread in the milk. Scoop out the roe from the skin into a liquidiser. Add the onion, olive oil and lemon juice. Squeeze out the bread from the milk and add to the mixture, discarding the milk. Liquidise until smooth. Season with black pepper and garnish with parsley and green olives.

4 slices white bread
80ml/3floz milk
225g/8oz smoked cod roe
1 onion, chopped
150ml/¼pint olive oil
juice 1 lemon
black pepper
chopped parsley
chopped green olives

Smoky Corn Vol-au-vents

100g/4oz smoked cod
150ml/¼pint milk
½ green pepper, deseeded and
   finely chopped
15g/½oz butter
1 tablespoon flour
100g/4oz canned sweetcorn,
   drained
salt, pepper
8 medium, baked vol-au-vent
   cases

Poach cod in milk for 10 minutes and blanch the pepper in boiling water for 8-10 minutes. Drain fish, retaining the liquid it was cooked in and drain peppers. Melt the butter in a pan and stir in the flour. Add the milk from the cod and bring to the boil. Continue cooking for 2-3 minutes, stirring all the time. Add flaked cod, pepper and the sweetcorn. Season to taste and warm through. Pile into warmed vol-au-vent cases.

Golden Fish Flan

150g/5oz shortcrust pastry
175g/6oz smoked cod or
   haddock
1 small plaice, filleted
25g/1oz butter
25g/1oz flour
250ml/8floz milk
salt, pepper
8 cooked mussels
100g/4oz peeled prawns
½ packet potato crisps
25g/1oz grated cheese

Roll out the pastry and use to line a fairly deep 20cm/8in flan tin. Bake blind at 200°C/400°F/Mark 6 for 10 minutes. Poach or steam cod and plaice in separate pans. When they are cooked, drain and leave to cool. Melt the butter in a pan and add the flour. Stir well and gradually add the milk. Bring to the boil, stirring all the time, and season to taste. Flake the cod and use to line the flan case. Cut the plaice into small chunks and arrange in the flan with the mussels. Place the prawns on top. Cover with sauce. Crush the potato crisps and mix with grated cheese; sprinkle over the top. Bake at 200°C/400°F/Mark 6 for about 20 minutes until the top is crisp and golden.

Arbroath Smokies

450g/1lb Arbroath smokies
   (small, hot-smoked haddock)
300ml/½pint water
25g/1oz butter
25g/1oz flour
black pepper
50g/2oz grated cheese
lemon juice

Skin and bone the fish and retain the skin. Boil the skin with the water for 10 minutes, strain and reserve the liquor. Melt the butter in a pan and add the flour, stir well. Gradually add the fish liquor, stirring all the time. Bring to the boil and season with black pepper. Add the cheese, retaining a little for garnish. Flake the fish coarsely and add to the sauce with a dash of lemon juice. Pour into individual ramekin dishes and sprinkle remaining cheese on top. Place under the grill to brown and serve at once.

Smoked Trout Mousse

Mash the trout with a fork. Place in a blender with the white wine and blend until smooth. Mix the gelatine with the water in a cup and stand in a pan of hot water to dissolve. Whip the double cream until fairly stiff and mix with the trout purée and gelatine. Mix the egg yolks with the fish mixture and season to taste. Whip egg whites until really stiff and fold into the mixture. Spoon into a mould and place in the fridge to set. Turn out and serve with brown bread and butter.

1 large smoked trout (350g/12oz), skinned and boned
150ml/¼pint white wine
15g/½oz gelatine
2 tablespoons water
150ml/¼pint double cream
3 eggs, separated
salt, black pepper

Smoked Eel Pâté

Mince the eel with the olives. Melt the butter and stir into the minced fish. Add lemon juice and season with black pepper. Spoon into a pâté dish and place in the fridge to set. Serve with hot toast.

225g/8oz piece smoked eel, skinned and boned
16 stuffed olives
100g/4oz butter
2 teaspoons lemon juice
black pepper

South African Fish Balls with Deep Fried Parsley and Celery

Melt the butter in a pan and stir in the flour. Gradually add the milk, stirring all the time. Bring to the boil, remove from the heat and add the egg. Flake the fish and mash with a fork. Add the fish, capers, breadcrumbs and seasonings to the sauce and mix well. Leave to cool. Shape into 20 small balls, coat in the beaten egg and then breadcrumbs. Deep fry in hot cooking oil until golden brown. Drain well and keep warm. Dredge the parsley and celery tops with flour and plunge into hot fat. Cook for 1 minute and remove. Drain on kitchen paper and serve with the fish balls.

25g/1oz butter
25g/1oz flour
150ml/¼pint milk
1 egg
175g/6oz cooked grey mullet or huss
1 teaspoon capers, finely chopped
50g/2oz breadcrumbs
salt, pepper, nutmeg
1 egg, beaten
dry breadcrumbs
oil for deep frying
50g/2oz mixed sprigs parsley and celery tops
flour

Eggs Léontine

100g/4oz haddock or huss
  fillets
fish stock
1 bay leaf
50g/2oz mushrooms, finely
  chopped
25g/1oz breadcrumbs
5 tablespoons double cream
salt, pepper
4 eggs

Poach the haddock fillets in stock with the bay leaf for about 8-10 minutes until cooked. Drain fish, flake and mash with a fork. Add the mushrooms to the fish with the breadcrumbs and 1 tablespoon cream. Season and divide into 4 portions. Place each portion in an individual ramekin dish. Break an egg into each dish and top with cream. Place the dishes on a baking tray and cook at 200°C/400°F/Mark 6 for 15 minutes until the egg whites are just set.

Marinated Cod with Chopped Gherkins

350g/12oz fresh cod, halibut,
  haddock or hake, skinned,
  boned and cut into chunks
juice 4 lemons
1 small onion, finely chopped
3 large gherkins, finely
  chopped
salt, pepper
3-4 lettuce leaves
cucumber slices

Completely cover the fish with the lemon juice. Place the onion and gherkins on top of the fish. Sprinkle with salt and pepper and place in the fridge for at least 4 hours. Serve on a bed of lettuce, garnished with cucumber slices.

White Fish Terrine with Fennel

350g/12oz huss
350g/12oz cod
150ml/¼pint milk or milk and
  water
1 small onion, sliced
1 blade mace
1 bay leaf
salt, pepper
50g/2oz breadcrumbs
1 egg
¼ teaspoon fennel seed
¼ teaspoon dried mixed herbs

Poach the fish in the milk or milk and water with the onion, mace, bay leaf and seasoning for labout 8-10 minutes or until tender. Remove the huss from the pan and take the flesh off the bone. Mash with a fork and mix with breadcrumbs and egg. Season well. Thoroughly grease a small terrine and pack half of the mixture into the base of it. Take the cod from the cooking liquor and remove any skin or bones. Flake the flesh into small chunks and arrange on top of the huss, pressing down well into the mixture. Sprinkle with fennel seed, herbs and seasoning. Place the remaining huss mixture on top and press down again.

Smooth over the top with a fork and cover with a lid. Bake in a tin of water at 180°C/350°F/Mark 4 for 1 hour. Allow to cool and turn out of the terrine. Serve in slices with fingers of thin brown toast.

Eastbourne Pâté

Poach the haddock in the milk and water with the tarragon and bay leaves. Remove the fish from the cooking liquor, discard the bay leaves and make the liquid up to 250ml/8floz with milk. Flake the fish and mash well with a fork. Keep on one side. Melt the butter in a pan and add the flour. Stir well and gradually add the milk and fish stock. Bring to the boil, stirring all the time, and cook for 2-3 minutes. Add the mashed fish, then the egg, and mix well. Season to taste. Grease a pudding basin and spoon the mixture into it. Cover with greaseproof paper and foil. Pour about 2.5cm/1in water into a large pan and place the basin in this. Bring to the boil and simmer for 45 minutes, topping up water if necessary. Remove from the pan and leave to cool. Chill and turn out on to a serving dish. Garnish with thin slices of cucumber.

350g/12oz haddock, skinned
150ml/¼pint milk and water
½ teaspoon dried tarragon
2 bay leaves
25g/1oz butter
25g/1oz flour
1 egg
salt, pepper
thin slices cucumber

Plaice Surprise

Grease 4 ramekin dishes. Roll up each fillet of plaice and lay one in each dish. Mix the egg with the milk, herbs and seasoning. Pour this mixture over the fish. Place the ramekin dishes in a tin with about 2cm/¾in water in the base. Bake at 180°C/350°F/Mark 4 for about 45 minutes until set.

4 plaice fillets
  (white-skinned)
1 egg, beaten
300ml/½pint milk
½ teaspoon dried tarragon
2 teaspoons chopped parsley
salt, pepper

Whitebait

Toss the whitebait in the seasoned flour. Heat the oil in a deep fryer until hot. Place small batches of the whitebait in the basket and deep fry for about 2-3 minutes. Drain and keep warm. Repeat until all the whitebait are cooked. Serve with lemon wedges.

600g/1¼lb whitebait
75g/3oz seasoned flour
oil for deep frying
lemon wedges

Devilled Whitebait

Dredge the fish in the flour and deep fry. Then dredge the onion rings in flour and deep fry too. Mix whitebait and onion rings and sprinkle on plenty of Worcestershire sauce. Serve with lemon wedges.

600g/1¼lb whitebait
100g/4oz seasoned flour
oil for deep frying
2 small onions, finely sliced
Worcestershire sauce
lemon wedges

Potted Shrimps

50g/2oz butter
salt, nutmeg, cayenne
600ml/1pint peeled shrimps
50g/2oz clarified butter
   (page 62)
3-4 lettuce leaves
lemon wedges

Melt the butter in a pan and sprinkle with salt, nutmeg and cayenne. Toss the shrimps in this until they are coated but do not cook at all. Pour into small moulds or dishes and leave to set. Pour the clarified butter over the top of each mould or dish to seal and keep in the fridge for up to 2 weeks. To serve, turn out on to a bed of lettuce and garnish with lemon wedges.

Prawn Cocktail

4-5 lettuce leaves
225g/8oz peeled prawns
2 tablespoons mayonnaise
   (page 66)
1 tablespoon tomato ketchup
juice 1 lemon
salt, pepper
lemon wedges

Shred the lettuce and arrange in the bottom of 4 individual dishes. Pile the prawns on top. Mix the mayonnaise, ketchup, lemon juice, salt and pepper to a smooth cream and pour over the prawns. Garnish with lemon wedges.

Prawn Royale

25g/1oz butter
25g/1oz flour
250ml/8floz milk
25g/1oz grated cheese
salt, pepper
100g/4oz peeled prawns
2 hard-boiled eggs, chopped
2 tomatoes, sliced

Melt the butter in a pan, add the flour and stir well. Gradually add the milk and bring to the boil, stirring all the time. Cook for 1-2 minutes and add cheese. Season to taste. Place the prawns in 4 individual ramekin dishes and cover with hard-boiled egg and tomatoes. Pour over the sauce and bake on a baking tray at 180°C/350°F/Mark 4 for 10 minutes. Serve with brown bread rolls.

Mediterranean Cocktail

½ small melon, peeled, sliced
   and cubed
175g/6oz green grapes, halved
   and deseeded
100g/4oz peeled prawns
¼ teaspoon dried basil
2 tablespoons mayonnaise
   (page 66)
salt, pepper

Mix the melon and grapes with the prawns. Sprinkle with basil and toss in mayonnaise. Season to taste. Spoon into individual glass dishes.

Seaside Pâté

Peel and chop the prawns and place on one side. Discard the heads and boil the shells in the water with the bay leaf for 10 minutes. Strain the liquid and use to poach the huss. When the fish is tender remove skin and bones, and mash fish well with a fork. Add the breadcrumbs and chopped prawns. Beat the cream until fairly thick and fold into the fish mixture. Season to taste and press into individual pâté dishes.

600ml/1pint unpeeled prawns
300ml/½pint water
1 bay leaf
225g/8oz huss
25g/1oz breadcrumbs
150ml/¼pint double cream
salt, pepper

Prawns and Lettuce en Cocotte

Layer the lettuce, tomatoes and prawns in individual ramekin dishes. Add wine and double cream and sprinkle with salt and pepper. Bake at 190°C/375°F/Mark 5 for 20 minutes. Serve with brown bread and butter.

8 lettuce leaves, shredded
2 tomatoes, skinned and
  chopped
175g/6oz peeled prawns
100ml/4floz dry white wine
150ml/¼pint double cream
salt, pepper

Prawns San Lucar

Empty the contents of the can of tomatoes into a pan and bring to the boil. Add the onion to the tomatoes and then the vinegar, fennel seed, marjoram and seasonings. Continue to simmer for 10-15 minutes. Brown the bread cubes in the oil. Add the prawns and the parsley to the tomato mixture. Heat through but do not cook. Mix three quarters of the crisp bread cubes with the prawn and tomato mixture. Grease a casserole dish and pour the mixture into it. Top with the remaining bread cubes and place under the grill for 3-4 minutes.

225g/8oz canned tomatoes
1 large onion, finely chopped
1 teaspoon vinegar
pinch fennel seed
¼ teaspoon dried marjoram
salt, pepper
100g/4oz wholemeal bread, cut
  into small cubes
oil for frying
350g/12oz peeled prawns
2 tablespoons chopped parsley

Piquant Prawns

Rinse the prawns in cold water. Remove any eggs from under the body but do not remove the shells. Melt the butter in a pan with the cooking oil. Fry the onion with the spices, Worcestershire sauce and seasoning until golden brown. Add the prawns and toss in the fat until coated all over and heated through. Do not allow the prawns to overcook. Place prawns on a serving dish and pour the lemon juice into the pan in which they were cooked. Heat through and pour all the pan juices over the prawns. Serve with lemon wedges.

1.2-1.7 litres/2-3pints
  unpeeled prawns
50g/2oz butter
2 tablespoons cooking oil
1 small onion, finely chopped
½-1 teaspoon chilli powder
1 teaspoon ground cumin
Worcestershire sauce
salt, pepper
juice 2 lemons
lemon wedges

Prawns in Whisky

25g/1oz butter
3 tablespoons cooking oil
6 spring onions or shallots,
    finely chopped
1 clove garlic, finely chopped
2 tablespoons chopped parsley
225g/8oz peeled prawns
1 tablespoon cornflour
2 tablespoons whisky
4 tablespoons double cream
salt, pepper
4 slices fried bread, crusts
    removed

Heat the butter and oil in a pan and fry the spring onions and garlic. Add parsley and prawns and toss in the onion mixture to heat through but not to cook. Mix cornflour and whisky to a smooth paste and add to the prawns, stirring all the time. As soon as the mixture thickens add the cream and reheat. Do not allow the mixture to boil. Season to taste and serve on rounds of fried bread.

Potted Crab

1 cooked crab
salt, black pepper
50g/2oz butter, softened
50g/2oz clarified butter
    (page 62)

Remove all the crabmeat from the shell and rub through a sieve. Season to taste with salt and plenty of black pepper and press into individual ramekin dishes. Spread the softened butter over the top of the crab. Cover loosely with foil and bake at 180°C/ 350°F/Mark 4 for 30 minutes. Remove from the oven and leave to cool. Pour the clarified butter over the top of the cold crab, making sure that each pot is completely covered. Place in the fridge and eat within 2 weeks.

Crab Cakes

175g/6oz mashed potato
225g/8oz mixed crabmeat
50g/2oz breadcrumbs
25g/1oz grated Parmesan
    cheese
2 tablespoons double cream
2 tablespoons medium dry
    sherry
salt, pepper
1 egg, beaten
dry breadcrumbs
oil for frying
4 tomatoes, halved
sprigs parsley

Mix the mashed potato, crabmeat and breadcrumbs in a bowl and add cheese, cream and sherry. Season to taste. Shape into 8 or 12 small cakes. Dip each cake in the egg and then in breadcrumbs and fry in cooking oil. Grill or fry the tomatoes at the same time. Serve on a large plate decorated with parsley.

Crab Mousse

Melt the butter in a pan and add the flour. Stir and gradually add the milk. Bring to the boil, stirring all the time. When the mixture thickens, add the crabmeat and mayonnaise and mix well. Mix gelatine in a cup with white wine and stand in a pan of hot water to dissolve. Whip the cream and fold into the crab mixture. Add the gelatine, celery salt and black pepper and spoon into a 600ml/1pint mould. Place in the fridge to set. Turn out and serve with brown bread and butter.

15g/½oz butter
15g/½oz flour
150ml/¼pint milk
225g/8oz mixed crabmeat
150ml/¼pint mayonnaise
15g/½oz gelatine
3 tablespoons white wine
150ml/¼pint double cream
½ teaspoon celery salt
black pepper

Crab Cocktail

Divide the crabmeat into 4 portions, taking care to break it up as little as possible. Place each portion in a glass bowl. Mix the mayonnaise, ketchup, Worcestershire sauce, vinegar and pepper and pour over the top. Serve with wedges of lemon and brown bread and butter.

350g/12oz white crabmeat
3 tablespoons mayonnaise
  (page 66)
1 teaspoon tomato ketchup
½ teaspoon Worcestershire
  sauce
1 tablespoon tarragon vinegar
black pepper
lemon wedges

Avocado with Crab

Scoop the flesh from the avocados and place in a basin with half the lemon juice. Rub remaining lemon juice round the inside of the empty avocado skins and place on one side. Chop avocado flesh and mix with crabmeat, parsley, cumin, salt, pepper and mayonnaise. Spoon back into the avocado skins and serve on a bed of lettuce garnished with tomatoes.

2 avocados, halved and stoned
juice 1 lemon
100g/4oz mixed crabmeat
2 tablespoons chopped parsley
½ teaspoon ground cumin
salt, pepper
2 tablespoons mayonnaise
  (page 66)
4 large lettuce leaves
2 tomatoes, quartered

Avocado Royale

100g/4oz dark crabmeat
1 lump stem ginger in syrup,
  finely chopped
1 stick celery, trimmed and
  finely chopped
3 teaspoons double cream
salt, pepper
2 large or 4 small avocados,
  halved and stoned
100g/4oz white crabmeat
4-8 lettuce leaves
lemon wedges

Mix dark crabmeat with finely chopped ginger and celery. Moisten with cream and season to taste. Pile the crab mixture into the centres of the avocados. Spoon the white crabmeat over the top and serve on a bed of lettuce with lemon wedges.

Crab Suzanna

1 onion, finely chopped
25g/1oz butter
175g/6oz canned white
  crabmeat, drained
2 hard-boiled eggs, chopped
2 tablespoons chopped parsley
1 teaspoon Worcestershire
  sauce
1 teaspoon prepared mustard
¼ teaspoon cayenne
3 tablespoons double cream
salt, black pepper
50g/2oz brown breadcrumbs

Fry the onion in a little of the butter. Flake the crabmeat and remove any membranes. Mix the hard-boiled eggs with the crabmeat, onion, parsley, Worcestershire sauce, mustard and cayenne pepper. Fold in the cream and season to taste. Spoon into individual ramekin dishes and top with breadcrumbs and knobs of butter. Bake at 200°C/400°F/Mark 6 for 20-30 minutes until crisp and brown on top.

Salmon Pâté

200g/7oz canned salmon
milk
25g/1oz butter
25g/1oz flour
1 egg
salt, pepper
sprigs parsley

Drain the salmon, retaining the liquid. Mash salmon well with a fork. Make the liquid up to 300ml/½pint with milk. Melt the butter in a pan and add the flour. Stir well and gradually add the milk and salmon liquid. Bring to the boil, stirring all the time. Continue to cook for 3-4 minutes. Remove from the heat and add the mashed salmon and the egg. Mix well and season to taste. Grease a pudding basin and pour the mixture into it. Cover with greaseproof paper and foil. Place the basin in a pan containing about 2.5cm/1in water and bring to the boil. Cover with a lid, reduce the heat and continue to simmer for 40 minutes, topping up water if necessary. Remove the basin from the pan and leave to cool. Chill for 2 hours and turn out on to a serving plate. Garnish with parsley sprigs.

Salmon and Cucumber Pâté

Place the cubed cucumber in a bowl. Sprinkle with salt and leave to stand for 30 minutes. Rinse under running water and dry on kitchen paper. Flake the salmon with a fork and melt the butter in a saucepan. Place salmon, melted butter and cucumber in a blender and blend until smooth. Add curd cheese and pepper and blend again. Pour into a pudding basin or terrine and leave in the fridge for 2 hours to set. Spoon on to a bed of lettuce and decorate with thinly sliced cucumber. Serve with fingers of brown toast.

½ medium cucumber, cubed
salt
200g/7oz canned salmon, drained
75g/3oz butter
100g/4oz curd cheese
black pepper
4 lettuce leaves
thin slices cucumber

Scallops with Duchesse Potatoes

Boil the potatoes in lightly salted water until cooked. Mash and mix with half the butter and the egg. Season to taste. Reserve the shells and cut away any small black bits from the scallops and chop up roughly. Place mushrooms, scallops, onion and parsley in a pan with the water and wine and bring to the boil. Simmer for 2 minutes, strain. Reserve the liquor and set aside the contents of the strainer.

Melt the remaining butter in a pan and add the flour. Stir well and add the reserved liquor. Bring to the boil, stirring all the time. Add the scallops and mushroom mixture, removing the sprig of parsley, and then add the cream. Adjust seasoning. Pipe the potato mixture as a thick border round 4 of the largest scallop shells and pour the sauce into the centres. Mix Parmesan and breadcrumbs and sprinkle on the sauce but not on the potatoes. Dot with butter and set on a baking tray. Bake in the top of the oven at 180°C/350°F/Mark 4 for 15-20 minutes.

225g/8oz potatoes
50g/2oz butter
1 egg
salt, pepper
6 scallops
100g/4oz button mushrooms, sliced
1 small onion, grated
1 sprig parsley
150ml/¼pint water or fish stock
150ml/¼pint dry white wine
25g/1oz flour
80ml/3floz single cream

Topping
25g/1oz grated Parmesan cheese
15g/½oz breadcrumbs
butter

Devilled Scallops

Poach the scallops in the milk and water for about 4-5 minutes until tender. Drain and chop the scallops and place in a pan with the cream, mustard, anchovy essence, Worcestershire sauce and seasoning. Stir over a gentle heat until heated through. Do not allow the mixture to boil. Spoon the mixture into 4 scallop shells and sprinkle with the breadcrumbs. Dot with butter and place under a hot grill until the top is lightly browned.

12 scallops
150ml/¼pint milk and water
150ml/¼pint double cream
2 teaspoons French mustard
1 teaspoon anchovy essence
½ teaspoon Worcestershire sauce
salt, pepper
4 tablespoons breadcrumbs
15g/½oz butter

Smoked Salmon and Egg Tarts

175g/6oz shortcrust pastry
50g/2oz frozen peas
sprigs watercress

Filling
4 eggs, beaten
2 tablespoons milk
butter
100g/4oz smoked salmon,
   diced
salt, pepper

Roll out the pastry and use to line 12 tartlet tins. Prick the bases with a fork. Fill with foil and dry beans and bake at 200°C/400°F/Mark 6 for about 10 minutes. Remove the foil and beans and continue cooking until golden in colour. Remove from the tins and place on a wire rack to cool. Cook the peas as directed on the packet.

To make filling, scramble the eggs with the milk and knob of butter until soft and creamy. Remove from the heat and leave to cool in the pan, stirring from time to time. Take care not to over-cook the eggs. Mix the smoked salmon with the cold scrambled eggs and season to taste. Spoon the mixture into the tartlets and decorate with cold peas. Serve garnished with watercress.

Smoked Salmon Pâté in Aspic

225g/8oz smoked salmon bits,
   minced
75g/3oz butter, softened
4 tablespoons double cream
1 tablespoon lemon juice
black pepper
150ml/¼pint aspic jelly

Mix the smoked salmon with softened butter. Add cream, lemon juice and black pepper and mix well together. Spoon into individual pots and place in the fridge to chill. After about 2-3 hours turn out the pâté and coat with aspic. Return to the fridge to set fully. Serve with brown bread and butter.

6 Hot Dishes

Mackerel Parcels

Place each mackerel on a piece of buttered foil. Mix the garlic with the butter. Spread a quarter of this mixture inside and on top of each fish. Sprinkle with salt and pepper and wrap up the fish, making sure that there are no holes for the steam to escape. Place the parcels on a baking tray and cook at 180°C/350°F/ Mark 4 for 30 minutes. Serve in the foil and open at the table.

4 small mackerel, cleaned
4 cloves garlic, crushed
100g/4oz butter
salt, pepper

Devon Mackerel

Place the mackerel in a casserole or ovenproof dish. Place some of the onion and apple slices in the centres of the mackerel and the remainder on top. Mix cider with marjoram and seasoning and pour over the fish. Cover with a lid or with foil and bake at 190°C/375°F/Mark 5 for 25-30 minutes.

4 mackerel, cleaned
2 onions, sliced
4 dessert apples, peeled, cored
  and sliced
150ml/¼pint dry cider
1 teaspoon dried marjoram
salt, pepper

Poached Mackerel with Lemon and Gooseberry Sauce

Place the mackerel in a pan and cover with water. Add the onion, carrot and bay leaf. Season and bring to the boil. Turn down the heat and simmer for about 10 minutes until the fish are tender.

   Make the sauce by melting butter in another pan. Add the flour and stir well. Next add 150ml/¼pint strained fish stock from the mackerel and the cooked and puréed gooseberries. Bring to the boil, stirring all the time. Add chives, lemon juice and seasoning and cook for 5 minutes. Serve with the mackerel.

4 small mackerel, cleaned
1 onion, chopped
1 carrot, chopped
1 bay leaf
salt, pepper

Sauce
25g/1oz butter
25g/1oz flour
225g/8oz gooseberries, cooked
  and puréed
1 tablespoon chopped chives
juice 1 lemon
salt, pepper

Mackerel Adriatic

2 large or 4 small mackerel,
  filleted
½ cucumber, peeled and cut
  into long strips
1 teaspoon celery salt
½ teaspoon paprika
black pepper
2 onions, finely chopped
2 large tomatoes, skinned and
  chopped
1 small green pepper, deseeded
  and finely chopped
2 cloves garlic, finely chopped
oil for frying
2 rashers streaky bacon, diced
200ml/6floz dry white wine
3 tablespoons single cream

Grease a casserole dish. Place half the mackerel in the base of the dish and fill up the gaps between the fillets with some of the cucumber. Sprinkle with celery salt, paprika and black pepper. Fry the onions, tomatoes, green pepper and garlic in cooking oil. Add the bacon and cook until the vegetables are soft. Spread half this mixture over the fish and repeat the layers of mackerel and cucumber. Finish off with a second layer of vegetables. Pour the wine and cream on top. Cover and bake at 180°C/350°F/ Mark 4 for 35 minutes.

Baked Stuffed Freshwater Bream

1 large freshwater bream,
  cleaned

Stuffing
225g/8oz whiting, cleaned
25g/1oz bacon fat
2 rashers streaky bacon, finely
  diced
100g/4oz cooked rice
1 egg, beaten
¼ teaspoon dried mixed herbs
salt, pepper

Soak the bream in salt water overnight in the fridge. Wash and dry the bream. Make the stuffing by poaching the whiting and removing the bones and skin. Flake the fish and mash with a fork. Melt the bacon fat in a pan and fry the bacon. Drain on kitchen paper and mix with the fish. Mix in the rice, egg and herbs. Season to taste. Stuff the belly of the bream with this mixture and sew up the cavity. Place in an ovenproof dish and pour the remaining bacon fat over the top. Bake at 180°C/350°F/ Mark 4 for 45 minutes, basting every 10 minutes.

Potomac Pie

750g/1½lb potatoes
100g/4oz frozen peas
25g/1oz butter
3 tablespoons flour
500ml/18floz milk
75g/3oz cream cheese
425g/15oz canned mackerel
  in brine, drained and flaked
2 hard-boiled eggs, chopped
1 tablespoon chopped parsley
salt, pepper
butter

Cook the potatoes and peas separately. Drain and set aside. Melt butter in a large pan, mix in the flour and add the milk, stirring all the time until the mixture thickens. Add knobs of cream cheese and whisk into the sauce. Next add the mackerel, peas, eggs, parsley and seasoning and bring to boiling point. Turn into a hot casserole dish. Slice the potatoes and arrange on the fish mixture. Top with knobs of butter and brown under the grill.

Fish Kebabs (page 109)

Fish Cassoulet

Cook the beans in the same water for 1-1½ hours until tender. Do not add any salt to the beans as this tends to harden them. Drain and leave on one side. Fry the bacon, onion and leek in a little cooking oil until fairly soft. Skin and bone the fish and cut into small chunks. Layer with all the other ingredients in a casserole dish, seasoning as you go. Cover with a lid and bake at 180°C/350°F/Mark 4 for about 1 hour.

175g/6oz dried haricot beans, soaked in cold water overnight
3 rashers streaky bacon, diced
1 small onion, sliced
1 large leek, sliced
oil for frying
100g/4oz smoked cod
225g/8oz coley
1 small mackerel, cleaned
2 large tomatoes, skinned and chopped
salt, pepper

Choux Mountains

Heat the butter and water in a pan. When it is boiling remove from the heat, quickly stir in the flour and salt and beat well. Add the eggs one at a time, beating well between each addition. Place the mixture in a forcing bag and pipe out 8 mounds on to a greased baking tray. Bake at 200°C/400°F/Mark 6 for 45 minutes-1 hour until the outside is really crisp and the inside cooked through. Place the fish and leeks in a saucepan with half the milk, bay leaf and seasoning. Bring carefully to the boil, lower the heat and simmer for about 10 minutes until both fish and leeks are tender. Drain, and flake the fish. Melt the butter in a pan and add the flour. Stir well and gradually add the cooking liquor from the fish and the rest of the milk. Bring to the boil, stirring all the time, and cook for 3-4 minutes. Add the fish and leeks and adjust seasoning. Cook for a further 2-3 minutes.

When the choux pastry mountains are cooked, slit them three-quarters of the way round the centre and open up, taking care not to break at the back. Fill each with the fish and leek filling and close down the lid. Serve at once.
Note: Half the quantity of this recipe makes a good starter.

50g/2oz butter
300ml/½pint water
100g/4oz flour
salt
3 eggs

Filling
225g/8oz coley, cod or haddock, skinned and boned
450g/1lb leeks, sliced
600ml/1pint milk
1 bay leaf
salt, pepper
50g/2oz butter
50g/2oz flour

St Clement's Bake (page 112)

Fish Korma Curry

80ml/3floz yogurt
2 teaspoons ground cumin
1 teaspoon ground coriander
4 cardamom seeds
8-10 black peppercorns
2 cloves
750g/1½lb coley, cut into
  chunks
1 onion, finely chopped
1 clove garlic, finely chopped
oil for frying
1 tablespoon flour
¼-½ teaspoon chilli powder
4 tablespoons milk

Mix yogurt with cumin, coriander, cardamoms, peppercorns and cloves and pour over the fish. Leave to stand for 30 minutes. Sauté onion and garlic in cooking oil for 2-3 minutes. Add flour and chilli powder and stir well. Next add the milk and bring to the boil, stirring all the time. Pour on the fish and yogurt mixture and stir once. Bring to the boil. Turn down the heat and simmer very gently with the lid on for 8-10 minutes until the fish is tender. Serve on a bed of boiled rice.

Baked Whiting with Fennel

1kg/2lb whiting, skinned and
  filleted
salt, pepper
450g/1lb fennel
100g/4oz mushrooms
400g/14oz canned tomatoes

Season the whiting fillets and roll up. Arrange in a shallow oven-proof dish. Parboil the fennel for 6-8 minutes and cut into wedges. Place the fennel round the fish and slice the mushrooms over the top. Pour the contents of the can of tomatoes over the top of the fish. Season and cover with foil. Bake at 200°C/400°F/Mark 6 for 30 minutes.

Summer Stew

50g/2oz streaky bacon, cut into
  small pieces
3 onions, sliced
3 carrots, chopped
1 tablespoon cooking oil
2 large potatoes, diced
3 courgettes, sliced
3 tomatoes, sliced
300ml/½pint milk and water
1 bay leaf
salt, pepper
450g/1lb huss, boned and cut
  into chunks

Place the bacon, onions and carrots in a deep pan and sauté in cooking oil for 4-5 minutes. Add the potatoes, courgettes and tomatoes to the pan with milk and water, bay leaf and seasoning. Bring to the boil and simmer for 15 minutes. Add the fish to the stew and stir. Continue cooking until the fish is tender, about 10 minutes. Serve in soup plates.

Baked Garfish

Butter a casserole dish and lay the fish in the base of it. Sprinkle the bacon and green pepper over the fish. Season and add tomatoes. Cover and bake at 180°C/350°F/Mark 4 for 15 minutes. Mix soured cream with flour and gradually blend in the fish stock. Add herbs and seasoning and heat through. Pour over the fish and bake for a further 10 minutes.

2 garfish, cleaned, skinned and cut into steaks
2 rashers streaky bacon, diced
1 green pepper, deseeded and diced
salt, pepper
3 tomatoes, skinned and sliced
150ml/¼ pint soured cream
1 tablespoon flour
150ml/¼ pint fish stock
1 tablespoon chopped parsley
1 teaspoon dried rosemary

Stuffed Squid

Very finely chop the squid tentacles and mix with the mushrooms and breadcrumbs. Moisten with a little of the tomato juice. Add herbs and seasoning and stuff into the squid, taking care to push the stuffing well down inside the body. Secure with cocktail sticks and place in a casserole dish. Pour the remaining tomato juice over the top. Cover and bake at 190°C/375°F/Mark 5 for 25-30 minutes.

4 medium or 8-12 baby squid, cleaned
100g/4oz mushrooms, finely chopped
100g/4oz breadcrumbs
400ml/¾ pint canned tomato juice
¼ teaspoon dried oregano
pinch fennel seed
salt, pepper

Skate in Black Butter

Put the skate in a pan and cover with water. Add the onion, bay leaf, peppercorns, parsley and salt. Bring to the boil and simmer gently for about 20-25 minutes. Remove the fish and keep hot.

Heat the butter in a frying pan and cook over a low heat until browned, about 3-4 minutes. Remove from heat and stir in the lemon juice and chopped parsley. Pour over the skate.

4 skate wings
½ onion, sliced
1 bay leaf
4 peppercorns
1 sprig parsley
salt

Sauce
100g/4oz butter
1 tablespoon lemon juice
2 tablespoons chopped parsley

Skate with Onions

20 pickling onions
50g/2oz butter
4 skate wings
25g/1oz flour
300ml/½pint milk
2 cloves
1 bay leaf
¼ teaspoon dried thyme
salt, pepper
50g/2oz grated Cheddar cheese

Sauté the onions gently in half the butter until tender. Steam the skate wings. Melt the remaining butter in a pan and add the flour. Stir well and gradually add the milk. Add cloves, bay leaf, thyme and seasoning. Bring to the boil, stirring all the time. Cook for 2-3 minutes. Add cheese and heat through. Arrange skate on a large serving dish and sprinkle the onions over it. Strain sauce to remove cloves and bay leaf and pour over the top. Serve at once.

Conger Eel with Green Pepper

50g/2oz butter
50g/2oz flour
600ml/1pint dry cider
salt, pepper
1kg/2lb conger eel, skinned, boned and cut into chunks
100g/4oz mushrooms, quartered
1 green pepper, deseeded and chopped

Melt the butter in a pan and add the flour. Stir and gradually add the cider. Bring to the boil, stirring all the time, and season to taste. Mix fish, mushrooms and pepper in a casserole dish and pour the sauce over the top. Cover and bake at 180°C/ 350°F/Mark 4 for about 1 hour.

Baked Tuna Loaf

1 tablespoon minced onion
2 tablespoons cooking oil
2 tablespoons flour
250ml/8fl oz milk
1 tablespoon lemon juice
1 teaspoon Worcestershire sauce
200g/7oz canned tuna, drained and flaked
1 egg, separated
75g/3oz fresh breadcrumbs
salt, pepper
2 tablespoons dry breadcrumbs

Fry the onion in oil until golden brown. Add the flour and stir well. Gradually add the milk, stirring all the time. Bring to the boil and add lemon juice and Worcestershire sauce. Add the tuna to the sauce, then the egg yolk and fresh breadcrumbs. Mix thoroughly and season to taste. Shape into a loaf and place on a greased baking tray. Mix the egg white with a little oil and brush the loaf with this mixture. Sprinkle with dry breadcrumbs and bake at 200°C/400°F/Mark 6 for 30 minutes. Serve with cheese sauce or tomato sauce (**pages 62 and 66**).

Pasta Pescatori

Cook the pasta shells in lightly salted water until just tender. Drain and toss in butter. Flake the tuna and add to the pasta with the prawns, parsley and lemon rind. Next add the cream and seasoning and toss over a low heat until thoroughly heated. Do not allow to boil.

225g/8oz pasta shells
25g/1oz butter
225g/8oz canned tuna, drained
225g/8oz peeled prawns
2 tablespoons chopped parsley
grated rind ½ lemon
250ml/8floz double cream
salt, pepper

Baked Herrings Provençale

Make light slashes in each side of the fish with a sharp knife and season well. Sauté the onion and garlic in half the butter for 5 minutes. Place the tomatoes in the base of a shallow earthenware dish. Sprinkle with sautéed onions, garlic, herbs, sugar and seasoning. Pour on the vinegar, arrange the herrings on the top of this base. Dot with remaining butter and cover with foil. Bake at 190°C/375°F/Mark 5 for 30 minutes.

4 large or 8 small herrings, cleaned
salt, pepper
1 onion, finely chopped
1 clove garlic, finely chopped
25g/1oz butter
450g/1lb tomatoes, skinned and coarsely chopped
1 teaspoon dried Provençale herbs
1 teaspoon sugar
2 tablespoons wine vinegar

Herrings in Red Wine

Spread the mustard over the flesh of each herring and sprinkle with herbs and seasoning. Roll up with the skin on the inside. Place the rolls in a lidded casserole dish just large enough to hold them and pour the red wine over the top. Cover and bake at 190°C/375°F/Mark 5 for 20 minutes.

1 tablespoon French mustard
4 large or 8 small herrings, split and boned
1 tablespoon chopped parsley
1 teaspoon dried thyme
salt, pepper
150ml/¼pint red wine

Deauville Herrings

Sauté the cooking apples and onions in butter until fairly soft and add the marjoram and seasoning. Grease a large, shallow earthenware dish and place 4 of the herring fillets in it. Spread the apple and onion mixture over each one. Top with the remaining fillets. Pour on the cider and cover with foil. Bake at 180°C/350°F/Mark 4 for 15 minutes or until the herrings are cooked through.

2 cooking apples, peeled, cored and sliced
2 onions, sliced
25g/1oz butter
½ teaspoon dried marjoram
salt, pepper
8 small herrings, split and boned
3 tablespoons cider

Fish and Spinach Pancakes

Pancakes
100g/4oz flour
salt
1 egg
300ml/½pint milk
oil for frying

Filling
50g/2oz butter
50g/2oz flour
600ml/1pint milk
225g/8oz frozen spinach purée,
    thawed and drained
salt, pepper
225g/8oz cooked smoked fish
    (haddock, cod, mackerel,
    kippers)
25g/1oz grated cheese

Sift flour and salt into a basin and add the egg and half the milk. Beat well with a fork and then add remaining milk and leave to stand for 30 minutes. Use this batter to make 8 pancakes allowing a little over 3 tablespoonfuls for each. Place the pancakes on a plate and keep warm.

Make the filling by melting the butter in a pan. Add the flour, stir well and gradually add the milk. Bring to the boil stirring all the time. Cook for 2-3 minutes then divide into 2. Mix the spinach with half the sauce. Heat through and season to taste. Mix the remaining half of the sauce with the cooked smoked fish. Heat through and season to taste. Lay one pancake on a plate and spoon on a little of the smoked fish mixture. Top with another pancake and spoon on a little of the spinach mixture. Continue layering pancakes and alternate sauces ending with the spinach sauce. Sprinkle with grated cheese and quickly brown under the grill. To serve, cut like a cake into slices.

Kedgeree

2 hard-boiled eggs, chopped
450g/1lb cooked smoked
    haddock or cod, skinned,
    boned and flaked
225g/8oz cooked rice
2 tablespoons lemon juice
salt, black pepper, nutmeg
150ml/¼pint single cream
50g/2oz butter
2 tablespoons chopped parsley

Mix the hard-boiled eggs with the fish and rice. Add the lemon juice and seasonings, and stir in the single cream. Butter an ovenproof dish and turn the mixture into it. Dot with the butter. Bake at 180°C/350°F/Mark 4 for about 30 minutes. Stir in the parsley and serve.

Haddock Pudding

2 large onions, finely sliced
1 tablespoon cooking oil
3 large eggs, beaten
600ml/1pint milk
½ teaspoon dried marjoram
salt, pepper
6 slices bread, thinly buttered
350g/12oz haddock fillets,
    skinned and cut into chunks

Gently fry the onions in cooking oil until translucent. Mix the eggs with milk, herbs and seasoning. Layer the bread, fish and onions in an ovenproof dish ending with the bread, buttered side up. Pour over the egg and milk mixture and leave to stand for 30 minutes. Bake at 180°C/350°F/Mark 4 for 1 hour until well risen and crisp on top.
Note: This recipe is particularly good made with wholemeal bread.

Haddock au Gratin

Grease an ovenproof dish and lay the haddock fillets in it. Season with salt and pepper. Melt butter in a saucepan and add the flour. Cook gently for 2-3 minutes. Stir in the milk and bring to the boil, stirring all the time. Season with a pinch of nutmeg and pour over the fish. Sprinkle the cheese over the top and bake at 180°C/350°F/Mark 4 for 25-30 minutes until golden brown on top. The dish may be cooked with a piping of potato round the edge.

4 haddock fillets, skinned
salt, pepper, nutmeg
50g/2oz butter
50g/2oz flour
600ml/1pint milk
50g/2oz grated cheese

Grilled Sea Bream in Mint

Place the fillets on the grill pan, skin side down. Rub well with cooking oil and sprinkle with seasoning and mint. Grill until cooked, about 5 minutes, depending on the thickness of the fish. Place the fillets on a plate. Mix lemon juice with juices in the pan and pour over the fish. Serve at once.

4 sea bream fillets
2 tablespoons cooking oil
salt, pepper
2 teaspoons chopped mint
2 tablespoons lemon juice

Harlequin Fish Pie

Place the fish in a deep casserole dish. Add the onion, peppers, mushrooms and tomatoes to the fish with the peas. Melt butter in a pan and add the flour. Stir and gradually add the milk. Bring to the boil, stirring all the time and add seasonings to taste, and tomato ketchup, if used. Pour the sauce over the fish mixture and cover with a lid. Bake at 190°C/375°F/Mark 5 for 45 minutes.

450g/1lb cod, coley or
  haddock fillets, skinned and
  cut into chunks
1 onion, finely sliced
½ green pepper, deseeded and
  sliced
½ red pepper, deseeded and
  sliced
50g/2oz mushrooms, sliced
2 tomatoes, skinned and
  chopped
50g/2oz frozen peas
25g/1oz butter
25g/1oz flour
300ml/½pint milk
salt, pepper, nutmeg
1 teaspoon tomato ketchup
  (optional)

Bombay Bake

450g/1lb white fish (cod,
   haddock, coley, huss or
   whiting), cut into chunks
1 large pickled gherkin or small
   cucumber, diced
1 small onion, grated
1 egg, beaten
2 tablespoons chutney
3 tablespoons milk
salt, pepper
25g/1oz breadcrumbs
25g/1oz grated cheese
butter

Grease an ovenproof dish and place fish in the base of it. Mix the gherkin or cucumber and the onion with the egg, chutney, milk and seasoning and pour over the fish. Top with a mixture of breadcrumbs and grated cheese. Dot with butter and bake at 190°C/375°F/Mark 5 for for 35-40 minutes.

Fisherman's Hot Pot

100g/4oz canned tuna,
   drained
450g/1lb white fish fillets (cod,
   haddock, whiting or plaice),
   cut into chunks
450g/1lb potatoes, diced
1 large onion, finely sliced
100g/4oz button mushrooms
100g/4oz peeled prawns
25g/1oz butter
25g/1oz flour
250ml/8floz milk
salt, pepper

Flake the tuna with a fork. Arrange white fish, potatoes, onion, mushrooms, prawns and tuna in layers in a casserole dish. Melt the butter in a pan and add flour. Mix well and gradually add the milk to make a thick sauce. Season well and pour into the casserole. Cover and bake at 200°C/400°F/Mark 6 for about 1 hour. Stir and check that the potato and onion are tender before serving.

Fish Florentine

750g/1½lb white fish fillets
   (cod, haddock, plaice, huss
   or coley)
salt, pepper
juice 1 lemon
1 bay leaf
150ml/¼pint water
1kg/2lb spinach, washed and
   picked over
40g/1½oz butter
25g/1oz flour
200ml/6floz milk
25g/1oz grated cheese
1 teaspoon anchovy essence

Season the fish fillets and place in a shallow earthenware dish with the lemon juice, bay leaf and water. Cover with foil and bake at 180°C/350°F/Mark 4 for 20 minutes or until tender. Cook the spinach in a large pan in a little of the butter. Melt remaining butter in another pan and add the flour. Stir well and gradually add the milk and then the liquor from the fish. Bring to the boil, stirring all the time, and add the cheese. Adjust seasoning to taste. Place cooked spinach in the base of a casserole dish. Sprinkle with anchovy essence and then place the cooked fish on top. Pour the sauce over and glaze under the grill.

Oriental Fish Steaks

Fry the almonds with raisins in half the butter until light golden brown. Drain on kitchen paper and keep hot. Mix flour with cinnamon, salt and pepper and coat the fish with this mixture. Melt the remaining butter in the pan and add the fish steaks. Cover with a lid and cook slowly on both sides until done (about 5 minutes on each side depending on the thickness of the steak).

Meanwhile fry the onion in oil for 3-4 minutes. Add the tomatoes to the onion with remaining ingredients. Bring to the boil and simmer until soft. Remove bouquet garni. Liquidise or sieve the sauce and reheat. Place the fish steaks in a serving dish. Sprinkle with raisins and almonds and serve with the sauce.

50g/2oz blanched almonds
50g/2oz raisins
75g/3oz butter
2 tablespoons flour
¼ teaspoon ground cinnamon
salt, pepper
4 cod or hake steaks

Sauce
1 onion, finely chopped
oil for frying
450g/1lb tomatoes, coarsely
    chopped
1 tablespoon tomato purée
2 tablespoons sherry
1 bouquet garni
salt, pepper

Fish Kebabs

Thread skewers with mushrooms, cod, bacon, tomato, green pepper and plaice then repeat. Brush the kebabs with cooking oil and sprinkle with salt and pepper. Place under the grill and cook for about 8-10 minutes, turning from time to time. Serve with boiled rice.

100g/4oz button mushrooms
450g/1lb cod steaks, skinned,
    boned and cut into chunks
4-6 rashers streaky bacon, cut
    into squares
4 tomatoes, quartered
2 green peppers, deseeded and
    cut into squares
225g/8oz plaice fillets
    (white-skinned), cut into
    squares
oil for grilling
salt, pepper

Russian Cod

Place cod steaks in a pan with the gherkins. Pour on the juice and season. Cover with a lid and bring to the boil. Simmer very gently for 6-8 minutes. Drain and make up the liquid to 300ml/½pint with white wine. Keep the fish and gherkins warm. Melt the butter in a pan and the flour. Stir well and gradually add the liquid. Bring to the boil, stirring all the time, and cook for 2-3 minutes. Adjust seasoning to taste and pour over the fish and gherkins.

4 cod or hake steaks
8 large pickled gherkins or 4
small pickled cucumbers, sliced
150ml/¼pint gherkin or
    cucumber juice
salt, pepper
white wine
25g/1oz butter
25g/1oz flour

Cod Tortosino

4 cod steaks
1 chilli pepper, finely chopped
1 clove garlic, finely chopped
3 tablespoons cooking oil
4 tablespoons chopped parsley
100g/4oz ground hazelnuts
2 tablespoons flour
400ml/¾ pint milk
salt, pepper

Grease a casserole dish and place the cod steaks in it. Fry the chilli pepper and garlic in oil. Add the parsley and stir. Next add the hazelnuts and flour and stir well. Gradually stir in the milk. Bring to the boil and season to taste. Pour this sauce over the fish. Cover and bake at 180°C/350°F/Mark 4 for 20-25 minutes.

Cod Lyonnaise

2 rashers lean bacon, diced
3 rashers streaky bacon, diced
2 onions, coarsely chopped
750g/1½lb potatoes, chopped
4 tomatoes, skinned
  and chopped
3 tablespoons milk
350g/12oz cod steaks, skinned,
  boned and cut into chunks
salt, pepper

Fry the bacon gently in a deep pan. Add the onions, potatoes, tomatoes, milk, fish and seasoning. Bring to the boil and cover the pan with a lid. Turn down the heat and simmer very gently for 30 minutes. Stir from time to time and if the mixture shows signs of sticking add a little more milk.

Paella

oil for frying
4 chicken drumsticks, skinned
225g/8oz pork fillet, cubed
225g/8oz squid, cleaned and
  sliced
2 onions, sliced
1 clove garlic, sliced
2 red peppers, deseeded and
  sliced
225g/8oz rice
¼ teaspoon powdered saffron
4 tomatoes, skinned and sliced
50g/2oz frozen peas
chicken stock
salt, pepper
225g/8oz cooked mussels
600ml/1pint unpeeled prawns

Heat the cooking oil in a paella pan or large frying pan and fry the chicken drumsticks until brown and completely cooked. Remove the drumsticks and fry the pork cubes. When these are cooked keep with the drumsticks, fry the squid quickly and add to the meat. Add more oil to the pan, if necessary, and fry the onions, garlic and peppers for 5 minutes. Add the rice, saffron, tomatoes and peas and just cover with chicken stock. Add seasoning. Stir in the pork and squid and place chicken drumsticks, mussels and prawns on top. Cover with foil and cook very gently until all the liquid is absorbed.

Eels in Red Wine

Place eels and onion in a pan with the wine, lemon juice, bay leaf and seasoning and bring to the boil. Continue boiling fairly rapidly until the liquid is reduced by half and the eels are cooked, about 20-30 minutes.

750g/1½lb eels, skinned, boned and cut into chunks
1 onion, finely sliced
½ bottle red wine
juice 1 lemon
1 bay leaf
salt, pepper

Casserole of Eels

Scald the pieces of eel in boiling water for 30 seconds. Leave to cool. Dry, then season with salt and pepper and roll in flour. Place in the base of a casserole dish. Put the onion and tomatoes in a pan and bring to the boil. Add wine, oregano or marjoram and season to taste. Pour this mixture over the fish. Cover and bake at 190°C/375°F/Mark 5 for about 30-35 minutes. Sprinkle with freshly chopped parsley just before serving.

750g/1½lb eels, skinned, boned and cut into chunks
salt, pepper
flour
1 small onion, finely sliced
450g/1lb tomatoes, skinned and chopped
200ml/6floz red wine
½ teaspoon dried oregano or marjoram
chopped parsley

Monkfish with Capers

Roll the fish in seasoned flour. Melt the butter in a pan with the oil and quickly fry the fillets on both sides, about 4 minutes in all. Place the fried fillets on a heated serving dish. Add the lemon juice and capers to the frying pan. Heat through and pour over the fish. Serve at once.

750g-1kg/1½-2lb monkfish fillets, cut in half
4 tablespoons seasoned flour
50g/2oz butter
1 tablespoon cooking oil
juice 1 lemon
3 teaspoons capers

Roast Hake

Remove any fins and make a number of shallow slashes across the back of the fish about 3cm/1¼in apart. Place a tomato slice in each slash. Place the fish in a baking tin, dot with butter and sprinkle with fennel seed and salt and pepper. Surround with remaining tomatoes. Bake at 200°C/400°F/Mark 6 for 30 minutes basting once or twice.

1kg/2lb hake, cut in 1 piece
225g/8oz tomatoes, thickly sliced
butter
¼ teaspoon fennel seed
salt, pepper

Grilled Hake with Fennel

4 hake steaks
oil for grilling
½ teaspoon dried fennel
salt, pepper
4 tomatoes, halved
butter
3 bulbs fennel, trimmed and
 coarsely chopped

Rub hake steaks with cooking oil and sprinkle with fennel herb and salt and pepper. Sprinkle tomatoes with salt and pepper and dot with butter. Grill with the hake, which needs 5-6 minutes on each side depending on thickness. Plunge the fennel into boiling salted water and cook for 10 minutes until almost tender. Drain and chop finely. Mix with butter and black pepper. Arrange hake steaks in the centre of a warmed serving dish and place small mounds of fennel alternately with tomato halves. Serve with cream sauce or parsley sauce (**pages 62 and 64**).

Plaice McKenzie

10cm/4in length cucumber, cut
 into small sticks
100g/4oz peeled prawns
salt, pepper
3 large or 4 small plaice,
 filleted
250ml/8floz milk
40g/1½oz butter
40g/1½oz flour
80ml/3floz white wine
2 tablespoons double cream
chopped parsley

Mix the cucumber with the prawns and season lightly. Place a little of the prawn and cucumber on each plaice fillet and roll up. Place in a shallow ovenproof dish and pour the milk over the top. Sprinkle with salt and pepper. Cover with foil and bake at 180°C/350°F/Mark 4 for 20 minutes. Melt the butter in a saucepan and stir in the flour. Gradually add the liquid from the fish, keeping the rolled fillets warm. Add the wine and bring to the boil, stirring all the time. When the mixture thickens remove from the heat and add the cream. Pour this sauce over the fish and serve garnished with a little chopped parsley.

St. Clement's Bake

4 oranges
12 plaice fillets
salt, pepper
1 lemon

Peel and chop two of the oranges, removing all pith and seeds. Spread the chopped fruit over the fillets and roll up. Place in a casserole dish and sprinkle with salt and pepper. Slice lemon and another orange fairly thickly. Cut slices in half and wedge between the rolls of plaice. Squeeze remaining orange and pour the juice over the fish. Cover and bake at 190°C/375°F/Mark 5 for about 20 minutes until plaice is soft and tender.

Plaice and Prawn Roulade

Line a 25 x 35cm/10 x 14in Swiss roll tin with greaseproof paper. Oil the paper well. Melt the butter in a pan and add the flour. Stir well and add the milk, stirring all the time. Bring to the boil and cook for 1 minute. Remove from the heat and add the egg yolks and seasoning to the sauce. Whisk the egg whites until really stiff and fold into the sauce. Pour into the lined tin and quickly place in the oven. Bake at 200°C/400°F/Mark 6 for 15 minutes.

Meanwhile make the filling by melting the butter in a pan and making a sauce as above. Remove any dark skin from the plaice and cut the fish into cubes. Add to the sauce with the prawns and rosemary and heat through. Season to taste. Remove the roulade from the oven and pour two thirds of the fish sauce over it. Roll up, removing the greaseproof paper as you go. Serve with remaining sauce. Garnish with watercress.

Roulade
15g/½oz butter
15g/½oz flour
150ml/¼pint milk
5 eggs, separated
salt, pepper

Filling
50g/2oz butter
50g/2oz flour
600ml/1pint milk
450g/1lb cooked plaice fillets
175g/6oz peeled prawns
½ teaspoon dried rosemary
salt, pepper

Garnish
sprigs watercress

Stuffed Plaice

Slit the plaice along the backbone on the white side leaving 2.5cm/1in uncut at either end. Carefully insert the flat of the knife along each side and free about 5cm/2in of flesh on each side from the bones.

Mix all the stuffing ingredients and spoon a little of the mixture under each flap. Grease the fish with cooking oil and grill first the stuffed side and then the dark side for about 4-5 minutes per side depending on the size of the fish. Serve stuffed side up with mushroom sauce (**page 64**).

4 plaice
oil for grilling

Stuffing
25g/1oz breadcrumbs
1 egg
1 teaspoon anchovy essence
1 teaspoon dried mixed herbs
salt, pepper

Fruity Fish

Sprinkle the fish fillets with salt and pepper. Quickly sauté the bananas and the fillets in oil. Layer the fish fillets with the bananas in a casserole dish. Sauté the onion in the fat with almonds and raisins and place on top of the fish. Drain the pineapple chunks retaining 2 tablespoons of the juice to mix with the sherry. Add chunks to the casserole and pour the sherry mixture over the fish and cover. Bake at 180°C/350°F/Mark 4 for 20-25 minutes.

3 large plaice or sole, filleted
salt, pepper
4 bananas, sliced diagonally
oil for frying
1 onion, sliced
4 tablespoons flaked almonds
3 tablespoons raisins
225g/8oz canned pineapple
    chunks
2 tablespoons sherry

Egg Fried Fish with Sweet and Sour Sauce

2 large plaice, lemon sole or
    whiting, filleted and cut in
    half
oil for frying
2 eggs, beaten
50-75g/2-3oz seasoned flour

Sauce
225g/8oz canned pineapple
1 lump stem ginger in syrup
2 tablespoons wine vinegar
1 tablespoon brandy
1 teaspoon honey
1 teaspoon cornflour
150ml/¼ pint water

Garnish
lemon wedges
sprigs parsley

To make the sauce, chop the pineapple and place in a pan with the juice. Chop the ginger and add to the pan with 1 tablespoon of the syrup, the vinegar, brandy and honey. Mix the cornflour with a little of the water and add to the sauce with the rest of the water. Bring to the boil and simmer for 10 minutes.

Heat the oil in a frying pan. Dip the fish into the egg and then in flour and fry quickly on both sides until tender (about 3-5 minutes each side, depending on the thickness of the fillet). Serve on a warmed plate with lemon wedges and parsley sprigs.

Fritto Misto

450g/1lb mixed fish (filleted
    lemon sole, sprats, peeled
    scampi, and prawns)
75g/3oz seasoned flour

Batter
100g/4oz flour
salt
3 tablespoons oil
150ml/¼pint lukewarm water
1 egg white
oil for deep frying

Garnish
lemon wedges

Cut the sole into strips and wipe all the fish. To make the batter, mix the flour, salt and oil in a bowl. Add the water gradually to give a thick creamy consistency. Leave to stand for a least 2 hours. Whisk the egg white really stiffly and fold into the batter just before using. Toss the fish in seasoned flour and then dip in batter. Allow the excess batter to drip off and then deep fry in hot cooking oil for 2-3 minutes. Deep fry the fish in small batches. Drain and serve garnished with lemon wedges.

Baked Fish with Aubergine

Boil or steam aubergine for 10-15 minutes. Place 50g/2oz butter in a shallow earthenware dish and place in the centre of the oven at 180°C/350°F/Mark 5 until the butter melts. Dip the fish fillets in milk and then in seasoned flour. Place in the buttered casserole and baste well. Bake for 15 minutes, basting from time to time. Slice the cooked aubergine and dip in beaten egg and then seasoned flour and fry in the remainder of the butter until golden brown on each side. Remove the fish from the oven and arrange the fried aubergine round the edge and down the centre. Serve at once.

1 large aubergine
75g/3oz butter
3 lemon sole, filleted, skinned and cut into large pieces
milk
6 tablespoons seasoned flour
1 egg, beaten

Baked Lemon Sole with Pembroke Sauce

Roll up the fish fillets with the skin side inside, and place in an ovenproof dish. Pour on the fish stock and add the bay leaf and seasonings. Cover with foil and bake at 190°C/375°F/Mark 5 for 20-25 minutes until the fish is cooked. Very gently sauté the onion, leeks, celery and mushrooms in 25g/1oz butter. Continue cooking for about 5-8 minutes until soft. When the sole is cooked, drain off and reserve the liquid and keep the fish warm. Melt the remaining butter in a pan and stir in the flour. Add the liquid from the fish and bring to the boil, stirring all the time. When the sauce has thickened, add sautéed vegetables and adjust seasoning. Pour over the fish and serve at once.

4 small-medium lemon sole, filleted
400ml/¾pint fish stock
1 bay leaf
salt, pepper
1 onion, finely sliced
2 small leeks, trimmed and finely sliced
3 sticks celery, trimmed and finely sliced
12 button mushrooms
50g/2oz butter
25g/1oz flour

Georgian Baked Carp

Soak the fish in salted water for 3-4 hours before cooking. Parboil the potatoes and slice them. Grease a flattish ovenproof dish and arrange potatoes on the base. Drain and dry the fish and make sure all the scales have been removed. Place on top of the potatoes. Cover the fish with the tomatoes and dot with butter. Pour yogurt along the centre of the fish and round the outside on top of the potatoes. Sprinkle all over with salt and pepper. Cover with greased foil and bake at 190°C/375°F/Mark 5 for 45 minutes. Remove foil and serve.

2-2.5kg/4-5lb carp, cleaned
salt
450g/1lb potatoes
225g/8oz tomatoes, skinned and sliced
butter
150ml/¼pint yogurt
salt, pepper

Carp Medici

2-2.5kg/4-5lb carp, cleaned
salt

Stuffing
1 whiting, cleaned
fish stock
1 egg
25g/1oz brown breadcrumbs
½ teaspoon fennel seed
1 teaspoon dried fennel
½ teaspoon grated orange rind

Soak the carp in salted water for 3-4 hours before cooking. Meanwhile poach the whiting in a little stock. When it is cooked skin the fish and remove the flesh from the bones. Keep the liquor in which the whiting was cooked for soups or sauces. Flake the flesh well with a fork and mix with the remaining ingredients. Drain and dry the carp, making sure that all the scales have been removed. Fill the belly cavity with the stuffing. Oil a large sheet of foil and wrap the carp in this, sealing the ends well. Place on a baking tray and cook for 45 minutes at 190°C/375°F/Mark 5. Remove the foil and serve garnished with stuffed tomatoes and olivette potatoes (**page 72**).

Grey Mullet with Leeks and Lemon

1 large or 2 small grey mullet,
    cleaned and scaled
450g/1lb leeks, trimmed and
    finely sliced
1 small onion, finely sliced
grated rind and juice 1 lemon
150ml/¼pint fish stock
salt, pepper

Wash the mullet, making sure that all the scales have been removed. Place in a straight-sided ovenproof dish. Pile up the leeks and onion over the fish. Sprinkle the lemon rind on top and squeeze the juice into the dish. Add stock and seasoning. Cover with buttered foil and bake at 190°C/375°F/Mark 5 for 1 hour.

Baked Stuffed Mullet

1 large or 2 small grey mullet,
    cleaned and scaled
lemon wedges

Stuffing
450g/1lb whiting, cleaned
fish stock
100g/4oz breadcrumbs
2 tablespoons white wine
50g/2oz mushrooms, finely
    chopped
1 egg
¼ teaspoon dried rosemary
1 tablespoon chopped parsley
salt, pepper

Wash the mullet, making sure that all the scales have been removed. Poach the whiting in a little stock. When it is cooked, skin the fish and remove the flesh from the bones. Keep the liquor in which the fish has been cooked for soups or sauces. Mix the breadcrumbs with white wine and leave to stand for 20 minutes. Add the whiting flesh to the breadcrumbs and fork the mixture well. Add the mushrooms to the mixture with the egg, herbs and seasoning. Spoon the stuffing into the belly cavity of the mullet. Oil a large sheet of foil and wrap the mullet in it, sealing the ends well. Place in an ovenproof dish and cook for 1 hour at 190°C/375°F/Mark 5. Remove the foil and serve garnished with wedges of lemon.

Baked Stuffed Mullet (see above)

Baked Mullet Provençale

Wash the mullet, making sure that all the scales have been removed. Cut deep gashes into the back of the mullet and insert half a slice of lemon into each gash. Place the fish in a shallow earthenware dish. Sauté the onion, green pepper and garlic in oil. Add remaining ingredients and bring to the boil. Pour over the fish. Bake at 190°C/375°F/Mark 5 for 45 minutes, basting the fish frequently.

1 large grey mullet, cleaned
   and scaled
1 lemon, sliced
1 onion, finely chopped
1 green pepper, deseeded and
   finely chopped
1 clove garlic, finely chopped
oil for frying
225g/8oz canned tomatoes
2 tablespoons chopped parsley
½ teaspoon dried mixed herbs
salt, pepper

Noodles Amalfi

Cook the noodles in lightly salted water until just tender. Meanwhile melt butter in a pan and add the flour. Stir and gradually add the milk. Bring to the boil, stirring all the time, and add half the Parmesan cheese and season to taste. Drain the noodles and layer noodles, prawns, sauce, mozzarella and seasoning in a shallow earthenware dish ending with a layer of mozzarella. Sprinkle with remaining Parmesan and bake at 200°C/400°F/Mark 6 for 20 minutes.

175g/6oz noodles
50g/2oz butter
50g/2oz flour
600ml/1pint milk
50g/2oz grated Parmesan
   cheese
salt, pepper
450g/1lb peeled prawns
175g/6oz sliced mozzarella
   cheese

Prawn Curry

Fry the onion in the oil until soft. Add curry powder, cumin, cardamoms and flour and cook for a further 2 minutes. Stir in the prawns and add the stock. Add all remaining ingredients and bring to the boil. Cover and simmer gently for about 10-15 minutes. Serve with boiled rice.

2 small onions, finely chopped
3 tablespoons cooking oil
1 tablespoon curry powder
1 teaspoon ground cumin
3-4 cardamoms
1 tablespoon flour
350g/12oz peeled prawns
300ml/½pint chicken stock
juice 1 lemon
2 teaspoons apricot jam
225g/8oz canned tomatoes
salt, black pepper

Pasta Pescatori (page 105)

Prawn and Tomato Casserole

175g/6oz rice
2 onions, sliced
½ green pepper, deseeded and
    sliced
butter for frying
450g/1lb peeled prawns or
    scampi
300g/10oz canned condensed
    tomato soup
1 tablespoon sherry
150ml/¼pint single cream
salt, pepper, paprika
50g/2oz flaked almonds or pine
    kernels

Cook rice in boiling salted water for 10 minutes and drain well. Sauté the onions and pepper in butter. Place rice in a casserole dish with prawns and mix in all ingredients except nuts and paprika. Top the dish with these and cover with a lid. Bake at 200°C/400°F/Mark 6 for about 30 minutes, or until bubbly.

Green Peppered Prawns

2 small green peppers,
    deseeded and coarsely sliced
150ml/¼pint white wine
1 bouquet garni
salt, pepper
300ml/½pint milk
fish stock
25g/1oz butter
3 tablespoons flour
350g/12oz peeled prawns

Poach the green pepper in white wine with the bouquet garni and seasoning for 15 minutes. Drain peppers and keep on one side. Add the liquid the peppers were cooked in to the milk and make up to 450ml/¾pint with fish stock. Melt the butter in a pan and add the flour. Stir well and gradually add the milk and stock mixture. Stir until the mixture thickens. Add drained peppers and prawns. Heat through and adjust seasoning. Serve with boiled rice with pine kernels.

Prawns St. Malo

450g/1lb artichoke bases,
    quartered
25g/1oz butter
450g/1lb peeled prawns
2 teaspoons cornflour
150ml/¼pint double cream
1 tablespoon flaked almonds
salt, pepper
50g/2oz breadcrumbs
50g/2oz grated cheese

Gently sauté artichokes in butter. Add prawns and heat through. Drain off the juices and mix with cornflour. Return to the pan, stirring all the time. Add cream and flaked almonds and reheat. Do not allow to boil. Season to taste and turn into a casserole. Mix the breadcrumbs and cheese and sprinkle over the dish. Brown under the grill.

Trout with Orange

Lay the trout on a piece of foil large enough to enclose them completely. Cut one of the oranges into wedges and arrange in cavities of the fish. Grate the rind of the second orange over the fish and then squeeze the juice over them. Sprinkle with salt and pepper. Cover completely with foil, sealing up any gaps. Bake on a baking tin at 180°C/350°F/Mark 4 for 30 minutes. Do not open the foil until the dish is at the table.

4 trout, cleaned
2 oranges
salt, pepper

Trout Amandine

Roll the trout in seasoned flour. Melt 50g/2oz butter with the oil in a frying pan and cook the trout until golden brown on both sides. Remove to a serving dish and keep warm. Drain the fat from the pan and melt the remaining butter. Add the almonds and cook gently, stirring, until golden brown. Add lemon juice and parsley and pour over the trout.

4 trout, cleaned
seasoned flour
100g/4oz butter
2 tablespoons oil
4 tablespoons blanched
  almonds
2 tablespoons lemon juice
2 tablespoons chopped parsley

Lemon Trout

Place a little lemon rind inside each fish. Grill the fish for 5-8 minutes on each side depending on their size. Meanwhile whisk the egg yolks with the lemon juice, fish stock, sugar and seasoning, until light and frothy. Pour into a double saucepan and heat gently, stirring all the time, until the mixture thickens to the consistency of thick cream. Remove from the heat. When the fish are cooked remove the skin and coat each fish with the lemon sauce. Serve garnished with lemon wedges and parsley sprigs.

juice and grated rind 1 lemon
4 trout, cleaned
3 egg yolks
2 tablespoons fish stock
1 teaspoon sugar
salt, pepper
lemon wedges
sprigs parsley

Norland Trout

Place the trout in a shallow earthenware dish. Put a knob of butter in the belly cavity of each fish and sprinkle with herbs and salt and pepper. Pour the red wine down the sides of the dish and cover with foil. Bake at 180°C/350°F/Mark 4 for 30 minutes until the trout are cooked through. Serve in the dish in which they are cooked.

4 trout, cleaned
butter
2 teaspoons dried mixed herbs
salt, pepper
300ml/½pint red wine

Trout Provençale

1 onion, chopped
1 clove garlic, chopped
olive oil for frying
1 red pepper, deseeded and
    coarsely chopped
6-8 tomatoes, skinned and
    chopped
150ml/¼pint fish stock
¼ teaspoon dried thyme
1 teaspoon tomato purée
salt, pepper
4 trout, cleaned
chopped parsley

Sauté the onion and garlic in olive oil until translucent. Add coarsely chopped pepper, tomatoes, fish stock, thyme, tomato purée and seasoning. Bring to the boil and simmer for 15-20 minutes until all the vegetables are soft. Purée and return to the heat. The purée should be fairly thick. Poach trout and when they are cooked, drain and skin. Arrange on a serving dish and pour the vegetable purée over the top. Garnish with parsley and serve at once.

Trout in Sherry

65g/2½oz butter
2 cloves
1 small onion
5 sprigs parsley
pinch dried thyme
salt, pepper
3 tablespoons sherry
3 tablespoons water
4 trout, cleaned
15g/½oz flour

Melt 50g/2oz butter in a large pan with a lid. Stick the cloves into the peeled onion and add to the pan with 1 sprig parsley, thyme, seasoning, sherry and water. Place the trout in the pan and bring to the boil. Cover and simmer very gently until the trout are cooked, 11-15 minutes depending on the size of the fish. Mix remaining butter and flour to a thick paste. When the fish are cooked drain off the liquid and thicken with small balls of butter and flour, stirring all the time. Place the fish on a serving dish and skin. Pour the sauce over the fish and serve garnished with remaining sprigs of parsley.

Scampi Provençale

1 onion, chopped
2 tablespoons oil
450g/1lb peeled scampi
400g/14oz canned tomatoes,
    drained and chopped
150ml/¼pint dry white wine
salt, black pepper
2 teaspoons tomato purée
pinch dried mixed herbs
1 clove garlic, crushed
1 teaspoon cornflour

Fry the onion in oil until soft. Add the scampi and cook for a further 3 minutes. Add the tomatoes with wine, seasoning, tomato purée, herbs and garlic and simmer for about 10 minutes. Blend the cornflour with a little water and add to the mixture. Stir until thickened and cook for a further 2-3 minutes. Serve with plain boiled rice.

Scampi Meunière

Toss the scampi in seasoned flour. Melt 50g/2oz butter in a frying pan and cook the scampi until golden brown. Remove, keep warm and wipe out pan. Melt remaining butter and cook gently until browned, about 3-4 minutes. Add lemon juice, seasoning and herbs and pour over the scampi. Serve at once.

450g/1lb peeled scampi
4 tablespoons seasoned flour
100g/4oz butter
juice 1 lemon
salt, pepper
pinch dried mixed herbs

Baked Red Mullet

Make sure all scales have been removed from the fish. Sprinkle the inside of fish with fennel and seasoning. Fold each in oiled greaseproof paper and bake at 180°C/350°F/Mark 4 for 35 minutes for large fish and 25 minutes for medium fish. Strip the paper off the fish and serve with the liquor that has oozed from the fish mixed with heated lemon juice.

4 large or 8 medium red
  mullet, cleaned and scaled
1 teaspoon dried fennel or
  fennel seed
salt, pepper
juice 2 lemons

Goujons of Sole

Cut each half fillet into narrow strips. Coat the strips in seasoned flour, dip into the egg and roll in the breadcrumbs. Heat the oil in a deep fryer until hot. Fry the fish in batches for 2-3 minutes until golden brown. Drain and serve hot with tartar sauce (**page 68**).

3 Dover sole, filleted, skinned
  and cut in half
75g/3oz seasoned flour
1 egg, beaten
breadcrumbs
oil for frying

Fillets of Sole Bonne Femme

Grease an earthenware baking dish and put the fillets in it, each folded over once *en cravate*. Sprinkle mushroom stalks and shallots over the fish and season. Next pour on the wine and sufficient fish stock just to cover the fish. Add the herbs and cover with buttered foil. Bake at 180°C/350°F/Mark 4 for about 10 minutes. Sauté the mushroom caps in half the butter and the lemon juice. Remove the fillets from the liquid they were cooked in and arrange on a serving dish. Add the drained mushroom caps. Cover and keep warm. Strain the fish liquor into a pan and bring to the boil. Reduce slightly and thicken with the rest of the butter mixed with the flour. Bring back to the boil. Beat egg yolk with cream. Remove sauce from the heat and add the egg and cream mixture. Pour over the fish and mushrooms. Glaze quickly under the grill. Serve at once.

4 small Dover sole, filleted and
  skinned
100g/4oz button mushrooms,
  stalks finely chopped
6 shallots, finely chopped
salt, pepper
150ml/¼pint dry white wine
fish stock
1 bay leaf
1 sprig parsley
pinch dried thyme
50g/2oz butter
1 tablespoon lemon juice
25g/1oz flour
1 egg yolk
80ml/3floz double cream

Sole Véronique

3-4 Dover sole, filleted and
  skinned
150ml/¼pint water
150ml/¼pint dry white wine
4 peppercorns
½ onion, sliced
25g/1oz butter
25g/1oz flour
salt, pepper
2 egg yolks
100ml/4floz single cream
175g/6oz green grapes, peeled,
  halved and deseeded
chopped parsley

Butter an ovenproof dish and fold the sole fillets over in it *en cravate*. Pour over the water and the wine. Add the peppercorns and onion, cover and cook in the oven at 180°C/350°F/Mark 4 for about 15 minutes. Melt the butter and stir in the flour. Cook for 2-3 minutes. Strain the liquor from the fish and gradually add to the *roux*. Stir over a gentle heat until boiling. Season and remove from heat. Mix the egg yolks with the cream and add to the sauce. Thicken over the heat but do not allow to boil. Add the grapes, and pour over the sole. Sprinkle with chopped parsley.

Fillets of Sole with Cumin

3-4 Dover or lemon soles,
  filleted and skinned
300ml/½pint white wine
1 bay leaf
25g/1oz butter
25g/1oz flour
1 tablespoon tomato purée
1-2 teaspoons ground cumin
salt, pepper
3 tablespoons double cream
sprigs watercress

Poach the sole very gently in white wine with the bay leaf for 6-8 minutes until cooked. Place the fish on a serving dish and keep warm. Melt the butter in a pan and add the flour. Stir well and gradually add the liquor from the fish. Bring to the boil, stirring all the time, and add tomato purée, cumin and seasoning to taste. Simmer for 8 minutes. Add the cream, pour over the fish and garnish with watercress.

Sole Ravenna

3-4 Dover or lemon soles,
  filleted and skinned
fish stock
100g/4oz macaroni
100g/4oz button mushrooms
75g/3oz butter
50g/2oz flour
milk
60g/2½oz grated cheese
salt, pepper
100g/4oz peeled prawns

Poach the fish very gently in fish stock for 6-8 minutes until cooked. Meanwhile cook the macaroni in lightly salted water until just tender. Sauté the mushrooms in 25g/1oz butter. When the macaroni is cooked, drain and mix with the mushrooms. Place on one side and keep warm. Melt remaining butter in a pan, add flour and stir well. Make the fish liquor up to 600ml/1pint with milk and gradually add to the butter and flour mixture, stirring all the time. Bring to the boil, add 50g/2oz cheese and season to taste. Mix prawns with macaroni and mushrooms and place in a shallow earthenware dish. Arrange the fish fillets on top and pour the cheese sauce over. Sprinkle remaining cheese on the top and bake at 220°C/425°F/Mark 7 for 10 minutes until the top is lightly browned.

Sole Normandy

Season the fillets and roll up. Secure with a cocktail stick and place in a shallow earthenware dish. Pour over the cider. Cover with foil and bake at 180°C/350°F/Mark 4 for 10 minutes or until tender. Meanwhile cook the mussels (**page 44**). Melt the butter in a pan and add the flour. Stir well and gradually add the liquor from the fish. Bring to the boil, stirring all the time. Season to taste. Add the cream and pour over the fish. Shell the mussels and arrange mussels round the outside of the dish. Sprinkle with parsley.

3-4 Dover or lemon soles, filleted and skinned
salt, pepper
300ml/½pint dry cider
600ml/1pint mussels
25g/1oz butter
25g/1oz flour
salt, pepper
3 tablespoons double cream
chopped parsley

Sole Lavinia

Rub each fillet with lemon. Sauté mushrooms gently in 25g/1oz butter and leave on one side. Melt remaining butter in a pan and add the flour. Stir well and gradually add the milk. Bring to the boil, stirring all the time, and cook for 2-3 minutes. Add mushrooms, single cream, prawns and cheese and season to taste. Grease a casserole dish and place 2 fillets side by side in the base. Cover with sauce and add 2 more fillets. Continue adding sauce and fillets ending with the sauce. Top with breadcrumbs and knobs of butter and bake at 180°C/350°F/Mark 4 for 30-35 minutes.

4 Dover or lemon sole or plaice, filleted and skinned
½ lemon
100g/4oz button mushrooms, sliced
75g/3oz butter
50g/2oz flour
400ml/¾pint milk
150ml/¼pint single cream
100g/4oz peeled prawns or shrimps
25g/1oz grated cheese
salt, pepper
25g/1oz breadcrumbs
butter

Fillet of Sole with Calvados

Ask the fishmonger for the fish heads and backbones and simmer these for 15 minutes in the wine and water with bouquet garni and seasoning. Drain the liquid off and reserve for poaching the fish. Soak the grapes in Calvados for 1 hour. Roll up the fish fillets and poach in the reserved fish stock for 6-8 minutes. Remove the fillets and keep warm. Mix cream with cornflour. Rapidly boil the cooking liquor to reduce slightly and whisk in the cream and cornflour mixture. Add the Calvados and continue whisking until the sauce is creamy in texture. Add the grapes and heat through. Pour the sauce over the fish fillets and serve at once.

2 large or 4 small Dover or lemon sole, filleted and skinned
150ml/¼pint dry white wine
150ml/¼pint water
1 bouquet garni
salt, pepper
100g/4oz green grapes, peeled, halved and deseeded
4 tablespoons Calvados
4 tablespoons double cream
1 teaspoon cornflour

Halibut Montpelier

4 large courgettes
4 halibut steaks
1 tablespoon dry white wine
5 tablespoons fish stock or
  water
2 bay leaves
50g/2oz button mushrooms,
  finely chopped
6 tablespoons finely chopped
  chives
6 tablespoons finely chopped
  parsley
300ml/½pint soured cream
salt, pepper

Steam the courgettes in a little water for 8-10 minutes. Poach halibut in wine and stock with bay leaves for 8-10 minutes depending on the size of the steaks. Drain the courgettes and halve lengthways. Remove halibut steaks and arrange on a serving plate with courgettes. Keep warm. Add mushrooms and herbs to the halibut cooking liquor and simmer for 5 minutes. Add soured cream and seasoning and heat through. Pour the sauce over the halibut and courgettes. Serve at once.

Halibut Peking

4 halibut steaks
8-10 spring onions, coarsely
  chopped
2 lumps stem ginger in syrup
salt, pepper

Place halibut steaks on a piece of aluminium foil large enough to enclose them completely. Sprinkle spring onions on top of the fish. Finely chop ginger and add to the onions with 2 tablespoons syrup. Season and wrap completely in foil. Bake at 190°C/375°F/Mark 5 for 15-20 minutes depending on the thickness of the fish steaks. Open up the foil at the table.

Halibut en Croûte

400g/14oz puff pastry
4 halibut steaks
8-10 spring onions, finely
  chopped
50g/2oz butter, softened
4 tablespoons chopped parsley
salt, pepper
lemon juice
1 egg, beaten

Roll out the pastry into 4 rectangles each large enough to wrap up a halibut steak. Mix spring onions, butter and parsley in a basin and season. Place a halibut steak in the centre of each piece of pastry. Spread the onion and parsley mixture on top and sprinkle with a little lemon juice. Fold the pastry over each steak and damp the edges to seal the seam and the ends. Make 1 or 2 cuts on top to allow the steam to escape. Place the pastry parcels on a greased baking tray, brush with beaten egg and bake at 220°C/425°F/Mark 7 for 20-25 minutes until the pastry is golden brown and risen.

Salmon Cutlets with Cucumber Sauce

Place cutlets in a pan and just cover with water. Add the onion and carrot, bay leaf, oil and seasonings. Bring slowly to the boil and boil for 1 minute. Turn off the heat and leave to stand for 5 minutes.

To make the sauce, put the cucumber, yogurt and cornflour in a blender and blend until very smooth. Melt the butter in a small saucepan. Pour on the cucumber mixture and bring to the boil, stirring all the time. Continue to cook for 2-3 minutes and season to taste. Drain the cutlets and serve with the sauce.

4 salmon cutlets
1 onion, chopped
1 carrot, chopped
1 bay leaf
1 teaspoon oil
salt, pepper

Sauce
¼ medium cucumber, cubed
80ml/3floz yogurt
1½ tablespoons cornflour
15g/½oz butter
salt, pepper

Salmon Royale

Place salmon in a pan and just cover with water. Add the onion and carrot, bay leaf, oil and seasoning. Bring slowly to the boil and boil for 1 minute. Turn off the heat and leave to stand for 15 minutes.

Make the sauce by simmering the mushrooms in champagne for 10 minutes. Melt the butter in a pan and stir in the flour. Gradually add the strained champagne juice from the mushrooms, stirring all the time. Bring to the boil. Add cream and season to taste. Remove salmon from the cooking liquor and skin. Put on a serving dish with mushrooms and pour champagne sauce over the top. Serve at once.

Alternatively, the poached salmon may be served with hollandaise sauce (**page 63**).

1kg/2lb piece of salmon or
   salmon trout
1 onion, chopped
1 carrot, chopped
1 bay leaf
1 teaspoon oil
salt, pepper

Sauce
100g/4oz button mushrooms,
   quartered
¼ bottle champagne
25g/1oz butter
25g/1oz flour
4 tablespoons double cream
salt, pepper

Lobster Newburg

Remove the meat from the lobsters as indicated on **page 43** and cut into large chunks. Sauté in butter for a few minutes. Add the brandy and flame. Mix the egg yolks with cream. Place in the top of a double saucepan and cook over water, stirring all the time, until the mixture coats the spoon. Add the lobster meat, pan juices and seasonings. Heat through, taking care not to curdle the sauce. Serve on a bed of rice or fried bread, or in vol-au-vents.

3 cooked lobsters, split
   lengthways
50g/2oz butter
3 tablespoons heated brandy
2 egg yolks, beaten
300ml/½pint double cream
salt, pepper, paprika, cayenne

Lobster Thermidor

2 cooked lobsters, split
    lengthways
300ml/½pint dry white wine
300ml/½pint fish stock
1 onion, sliced
300ml/½pint milk
1 sprig thyme wrapped in leek
    leaves
salt, black pepper, cayenne
65g/2½oz butter
40g/1½oz flour
1 teaspoon prepared mustard
1 egg yolk
80ml/3floz single cream
50g/2oz grated Parmesan
    cheese
25g/1oz dry breadcrumbs
lettuce leaves

Remove the meat from the lobsters as indicated on **page 43**, and cut into large chunks. Rub any loose coral through a fine sieve and place on one side. Pour wine and stock into a pan and boil rapidly until it is reduced to 150ml/¼pint. Place the onion in another pan with milk, thyme, salt and pepper. Bring to the boil and remove from the heat. Leave to stand for about 20 minutes. Then melt 40g/1½oz butter in a pan and stir in the flour. Gradually add the reduced wine and fish stock and the strained milk, stirring all the time. Bring to the boil and cook for 2-3 minutes. Meanwhile melt the remaining butter and toss the lobster in it but do not allow to cook.

Remove lobster and sauce from the heat and mix together. Add cayenne pepper, mustard, sieved coral, egg yolk and cream and correct seasoning if necessary. Spoon the mixture back into the lobster shells. Mix Parmesan and dry breadcrumbs and sprinkle over the lobster mixture. Place under a high grill to brown. Serve on a bed of lettuce.

7 Cold Dishes

Pilchard Pie

Roll out half the pastry and line an 18cm/7in flan tin. Drain tomato sauce from pilchards and make a sauce by mixing flour and butter over a low heat and gradually adding the milk and the tomato sauce. Season to taste. Chop pilchards and place in base of the flan. Mix the potato and onion well together and season. Spread on top of the pilchards. Cover this mixture with the tomato sauce and sprinkle with savory. Roll out the remaining pastry to make a lid for the pie. Fork the sides and prick the centre to allow the steam to escape. Bake at 200°C/400°F/Mark 6 for about 1 hour until the pastry is golden. Allow to cool.

225g/8oz shortcrust pastry
225g/8oz canned pilchards in
    tomato sauce
15g/½oz flour
15g/½oz butter
100ml/4floz milk
salt, pepper
2 potatoes, grated
1 onion, finely chopped
¼ teaspoon dried summer
    savory

Sardine and Potato Pyramid

Boil the potatoes and leave to cool slightly. Peel and dice. Mix the onion with the potatoes, oil and wine vinegar and leave until cold. Add the hard-boiled eggs to the potato mixture and season to taste. Pile the mixture in a pyramid shape on a bed of lettuce. Arrange the sardines standing up against the pyramid. Sprinkle with lemon juice and parsley.

3 large potatoes
1 small onion, finely chopped
2 tablespoons salad oil
1 tablespoon wine vinegar
2 hard-boiled eggs, chopped
salt, pepper
lettuce leaves
250g/9oz canned sardines,
    drained
juice 1 lemon
3 tablespoons chopped parsley

Smoked Brisling Flan

150g/5oz shortcrust pastry
200g/7oz canned mackerel in
    tomato sauce
salt, pepper
100g/4oz canned smoked
    brisling in oil, drained
1 hard-boiled egg, sliced
350g/12oz canned asparagus
    tips, drained
4 stuffed olives, sliced
300ml/½pint aspic jelly

Roll out the pastry and use to line a 20cm/8in flan tin. Bake blind at 200°C/400°F/Mark 6 until golden brown. Leave to cool. Mash the contents of the can of mackerel with a fork and season to taste. Spread over the base of the flan. Arrange the smoked brisling in a radial pattern on top of the mackerel. Place a slice of hard-boiled egg between each brisling. Arrange the asparagus on either side of the brisling and decorate with olives. Make up the aspic and pour over the flan. Leave in a cool place to set.

Mackerel Pasties

1 large mackerel, cleaned or
    425g/15oz canned mackerel
    in brine or oil
stock
1 onion, finely chopped
100g/4oz mushrooms, finely
    chopped
oil for frying
225g/8oz potatoes, grated
½ teaspoon dried marjoram
¼ teaspoon celery salt
salt, pepper
300g/10oz shortcrust pastry

Cook fresh mackerel in a little stock until tender. Remove skin and bones and fork the flesh. If using canned mackerel, drain and mash with a fork. Sauté onion and mushrooms in oil until soft. Add the potato to the mackerel with the mushroom and onion mixture. Add marjoram and seasonings. Divide the pastry into 4 and roll out into oval shapes. Place a quarter of the filling on each one and join the pastry over the top, pinching it together between finger and thumb. Place on a greased baking tray and cook at 200°C/400°F/Mark 6 for 35-40 minutes.

London Fish Loaf

450g/1lb whiting
225g/8oz smoked cod
milk
40g/1½oz butter
50g/2oz flour
2 eggs, beaten
black pepper
cucumber slices

Poach whiting and smoked cod in a little milk. When the fish are cooked, leave to cool and then remove the skin and bones. Keep the cooking liquor for the sauce. Mash the fish with a fork and keep on one side.

Melt the butter in a pan and mix in the flour. Make up the cooking liquor with more cold milk to 300ml/½pint and gradually add to the flour and butter mixture, stirring all the time. When the mixture thickens, continue to cook for a few minutes then remove from heat and add the eggs. Next add the fish and black pepper. Grease a terrine or loaf tin and spoon the fish mixture into it. Place the terrine or tin in a tray of water and bake at 190°C/375°F/Mark 5 for 1 hour. Leave to cool. Chill in the fridge and then turn out on to a plate. Serve garnished with cucumber slices.

Horseradish Fish Salad

Mix the macaroni and fish. Mix horseradish, cream, mustard and vinegar and season to taste. Add to the fish and pasta and place on a large serving dish. Arrange the beetroot round the edge of the dish.

350g/12oz cooked macaroni
350g/12oz cooked white fish (huss, haddock, cod), flaked
75g/3oz horseradish root, grated
150ml/¼ pint double cream
½ teaspoon prepared mustard
1 tablespoon tarragon vinegar
salt, pepper
225g/8oz cooked beetroot, peeled and sliced

Oriental Fish Salad

Cook rice in lightly salted water. Poach coley in a little milk with cardamoms, bay leaf, salt and pepper. When it is cooked, drain and leave to cool. Skin and bone mackerel and coley and mash well with a fork. Mix with rice and all other ingredients and correct seasoning. Spoon into a bowl and garnish with eggs, lemon and parsley.

100g/4oz rice
450g/1lb coley
milk
3 cardamoms
1 bay leaf
salt, pepper
225g/8oz smoked mackerel fillets
25g/1oz raisins
25g/1oz flaked almonds or pine kernels
2 teaspoons ground cumin
pinch cinnamon
1 teaspoon dried marjoram
1 tablespoon mayonnaise **(page 66)**
1 tablespoon salad oil
1 teaspoon vinegar
salt, pepper

Garnish
2 hard-boiled eggs, thinly sliced
½ lemon, thinly sliced
chopped parsley

Mussels Renaissance

2.5litres/4pints mussels, well
   scrubbed
300ml/½pint mayonnaise
   (**page 66**)
2 cloves garlic, crushed
1-2 canned or bottled red
   pimentos, cut into thin strips
sprigs parsley

Cook the mussels (**page 44**). Leave to cool and remove the top shell. Arrange the mussels on a large plate. Mix mayonnaise with garlic and spoon a little on to each mussel. Lay the pimento strips on top. Garnish with parsley.

Mussel and Artichoke Vinaigrette

225g/8oz courgettes, thickly
   sliced
½ cauliflower, divided
   into florets
400g/14oz canned artichoke
   bases, drained
2 x 150g/5oz jars cooked
   mussels, drained
2 rashers lean bacon
80ml/3floz vinaigrette
(**page 68**)

Steam the courgettes and cauliflower in a very little salted water for 6-8 minutes. Drain and leave to cool. Arrange on a plate with the artichokes and mussels. Crisply fry or grill the bacon and dice. Sprinkle over the dish and spoon on the vinaigrette dressing.

Tuna and Tomato Mould

200g/7oz canned tuna, drained
   and flaked
150ml/¼pint tomato juice
150ml/¼pint double cream,
   whipped
1 teaspoon Worcestershire
   sauce
½ teaspoon dried oregano
salt, pepper
15g/½oz gelatine
4 tablespoons water
2 tomatoes, sliced
chopped parsley

Mix the tuna with the tomato juice, cream, Worcester sauce and oregano and season to taste. Mix gelatine with the water and dissolve in a basin over hot water. When the gelatine has dissolved mix into the tuna and tomato mixture. Pour into a wet mould and leave in the fridge to set. Serve garnished with tomato and parsley.

South African Jellied Tuna

Mix the tuna with the cucumber. Add mayonnaise, lemon juice, yogurt and seasonings and mix well. Mix gelatine with the water and dissolve in a basin over hot water. When the gelatine has dissolved mix into the tuna and cucumber mixture. Pour into a wet mould and leave in the fridge to set. Serve garnished with watercress.

200g/7oz canned tuna, drained and flaked
7.5cm/3in length cucumber, finely diced
1 tablespoon mayonnaise **(page 66)**
1 tablespoon lemon juice
2 tablespoons yogurt
salt, black pepper, celery salt
7g/¼oz gelatine
2 tablespoons water
sprigs watercress

Tuna and Chicken Salad

Oil and season the chicken and roast at 190°C/375°F/Mark 5 for 1¼ hours until cooked through. Leave to cool and then skin and take the flesh from the bones. Cut into pieces and arrange on a large serving dish. Place contents of the can of tuna, including the juice, in a blender with the milk. Blend till smooth. Mix with mayonnaise and season to taste. The mixture should be thick and creamy. If it is too thick to pour add a little more milk. Pour over the chicken and garnish with sprigs of parsley.

1.5kg/3lb chicken
oil for roasting
salt, pepper
200g/7oz canned tuna
150ml/¼pint milk
250ml/8floz mayonnaise **(page 66)**
salt, pepper
sprigs parsley

Kipper and Mustard Slice

Roll out half the pastry to make a rectangular shape about 25 x 15cm/10 x 6in. Place on a greased baking tray. Roll out the second half of the pastry to a slightly larger size and slice across the centre to within 2.5cm/1in of the edges in lines about 1cm/½in apart. Cook the kippers as directed on the packet. Remove from the bag, retaining the liquid. Mash the kippers and mix with the hard-boiled eggs. Melt the butter in a pan and mix in the flour. Add milk and liquid from the kippers, stirring all the time. When the mixture thickens add the eggs and kippers with the lemon rind, mustard, parsley and seasoning. Pile this mixture on to the pastry base and spread to within about 1cm/½in of the sides. Cover with the slashed pastry lid, sealing the edges with a little water. Brush with milk and bake at 200°C/400°F/Mark 6 for 30-40 minutes until the pastry is risen and golden brown.

225g/8oz frozen puff pastry
350g/12oz frozen kipper fillets with butter
2 hard-boiled eggs, chopped
15g/½oz butter
25g/1oz flour
80ml/3floz milk
1 teaspoon grated lemon rind
2 teaspoons prepared mustard
2 tablespoons chopped parsley
salt, pepper
milk

Kipper and Pasta Salad

100g/4oz macaroni or pasta
  shells
3 tablespoons salad oil
350g/12oz frozen kipper fillets
  with butter or 3 fresh
  kippers
1 bunch watercress, washed,
  picked over, and coarsely
  chopped
1 small pickled cucumber,
  finely chopped
1 tablespoon vinegar
salt, pepper

Cook pasta in lightly salted water until tender. Drain and mix with salad oil. Leave to cool. Cook kipper fillets as directed on the packet or poach the fresh kippers in a little water. Leave to cool and remove any skin and bones. Flake with a fork and mix with the cold pasta. Add the watercress and pickled cucumber to the pasta and kipper mixture with the vinegar. Season to taste.

Buckling and Beetroot Cream

1 large buckling, cleaned,
  skinned and boned
450g/1lb cooked beetroot,
  peeled and diced
4-5 large gherkins, diced
pinch summer savory
salt, pepper
150ml/¼pint soured cream

Flake the fish into fairly small pieces and mix with the beetroot and gherkins. Add savory and seasoning. Just before serving toss in soured cream and correct seasoning.

Buckling Salad

1 large buckling, cleaned,
  skinned and boned
2 hard, eating apples, cored
  and diced
4 sticks celery, trimmed and
  finely chopped
7.5cm/3in length cucumber,
  finely chopped
2 carrots, grated
2 tablespoons salad oil
1 tablespoon vinegar
salt, pepper
sprigs watercress
2 hard-boiled eggs, sliced

Flake the fish and mix with the apples, celery, cucumber, carrots, oil and vinegar. Season to taste. Serve surrounded with watercress and hard-boiled eggs.

Smoked Brisling Flan (page 130)

Soused Herrings

Open herrings out flat and season with salt and black pepper. Arrange a few onion rings on each herring. Roll each herring from head to tail and secure with cocktail sticks. Arrange in a shallow ovenproof dish and pour over the spiced vinegar. Bake at 160°C/325°F/Mark 3 for 30 minutes. Leave to cool in the marinade.

4 herrings or whitings, cleaned and boned
salt, black pepper
1 onion, finely sliced
600ml/1pint spiced pickling vinegar

Stuffed Rollmops

Unroll the rollmops and remove the onion slices. Chop onion slices finely with the celery and gherkin. Mix with potatoes, tomato purée and mayonnaise. Season to taste. Spread the mixture on the flat rollmops and roll up again, securing with a cocktail stick. Garnish with tomato.

4 large or 8 small rollmop herrings with onions
2 sticks celery, trimmed
1 large gherkin
4 cooked potatoes, diced
1 tablespoon tomato purée
1 tablespoon mayonnaise **(page 66)**
salt, pepper
1 tomato, sliced

Kebabs with Savoury Rice

First prepare the savoury rice. Boil the rice until tender. Drain, mix with oil and vinegar and leave to cool. Add the sweetcorn and celery to the rice. Season to taste.

To prepare kebabs, grill bacon and cut into squares. Leave to cool. Poach plaice very carefully until just tender and leave to cool. Assemble the kebabs using small wooden skewers. Make up 12 kebabs with pieces of bacon, green pepper, smoked shellfish and button mushrooms. Make up a further 12 kebabs using halved grapes, pieces of plaice, tomato wedges and prawns. Arrange the kebabs on top of the savoury rice and serve with green salad.

3 rashers streaky bacon
1 plaice fillet (white skinned)
1 green pepper, deseeded and chopped
100g/4oz smoked oysters or mussels
12 button mushrooms
12 green grapes, halved and deseeded
2 tomatoes, cut into wedges
50g/2oz peeled prawns

Savoury rice
75g/3oz rice
1 tablespoon salad oil
1 tablespoon vinegar
100g/4oz canned sweetcorn, drained
1 stick celery, trimmed and finely chopped
salt, pepper

Salmon Mousse (page 145)

Jellied Eels

1kg/2lb eels, cut into chunks
1 bay leaf

Put eels in a large saucepan with the bay leaf. Barely cover with water and bring to the boil. Boil for 30 minutes and turn into bowls. Leave to set. If the liquid does not set, drain it off and boil for a further 10 minutes or add a little gelatine.

Marinated Eels

750g/1½lb eels, skinned, boned
   and cut into chunks
1 bay leaf
½ teaspoon dried rosemary

Marinade
1 large onion, finely sliced
2 tablespoons cooking oil
150ml/¼pint wine vinegar
80ml/3floz water
1 bay leaf
½ teaspoon chopped mint
1 tablespoon honey
½ teaspoon garlic salt
black pepper

Place the eels in cold water with the bay leaf and rosemary and bring to the boil. Simmer gently for 20-30 minutes until the fish is tender.

Meanwhile sauté the onion in cooking oil. Add vinegar, water, bay leaf, mint, honey, garlic salt and black pepper and bring to the boil. Simmer for 5 minutes and remove from the heat. When the eels are cooked, drain and cover with the hot marinade. Leave to cool and then chill before serving.

Scaddies

175g/6oz smoked haddock
   fillets
milk
225g/8oz potatoes
25g/1oz butter
25g/1oz flour
½ teaspoon anchovy essence
½ teaspoon French mustard
1 tablespoon chopped parsley
salt, pepper
4 small hard-boiled eggs
1 egg, beaten
4 tablespoons dry breadcrumbs
oil for deep frying

Cook the smoked haddock fillets. Drain and make the liquid up to 200ml/7floz with milk. Boil the potatoes until just tender. Melt butter in a pan and add flour, stir well. Gradually add the milk and fish juice, stirring all the time. When the mixture boils add anchovy essence, mustard and parsley. Flake the fish and mash the potatoes. Mix well together with the sauce and season to taste. Leave the mixture to cool. Divide into 4 portions and, with floured hands, mould each portion round 1 of the hard-boiled eggs. Roll in beaten egg and then in breadcrumbs. Deep fry for 2-3 minutes until golden. Drain and cool. Serve whole or halved.

Chilled Haddock with Prune Sauce

Place the onion in a large pan with bay leaf and milk and water mixture. Season to taste. Poach the fish steaks in this for about 8-10 minutes depending on the thickness of the steaks. Leave to cool. Meanwhile drain the prunes and place in a pan with 80ml/3floz fresh water. Bring to the boil and simmer until the prunes are tender. Leave to cool. Stone the prunes and place in a liquidiser with the liquid they were cooked in and the fruit juices. Blend till smooth. Drain fish steaks retaining the cooking liquor for soups and serve with the sauce handed separately.

1 small onion, sliced
1 bay leaf
150ml/¼pint milk and water
salt, pepper
4 haddock, cod or hake steaks

Sauce
100g/4oz prunes, soaked in
    cold water overnight
juice 1 lemon
juice ½ orange

Fish Salad Mould

Soak gelatine in the water, then add to hot fish stock and stir until completely dissolved. Add white wine and season to taste. Pour the gelatine liquid into a 15cm/6in ring mould to a depth of 5mm/¼in. Chill until set. Next arrange half the haddock chunks, lemon rind and egg in the mould and cover with more of the gelatine mixture. Leave to set and repeat the process.

To make the filling, toss the haddock with onion and lemon juice. Season to taste. To serve, turn the mould out on to a serving dish and fill the centre with the fish mixture. Garnish with tomatoes and parsley sprigs.

15g/½oz gelatine
2 tablespoons water
400ml/¾pint well-strained fish
    stock
80ml/3floz white wine
salt, pepper
225g/8oz cooked, smoked had-
    dock or cod, cut into chunks
rind ½ lemon, cut into thin
    strips
1 hard-boiled egg, chopped
2 small, firm tomatoes,
    quartered
sprigs parsley

Filling
225g/8oz cooked, smoked had-
    dock or cod, cut into chunks
1 small onion, finely sliced
juice ½ lemon
salt, pepper

Cold Fish with Lemon Sauce

Fry the onion in cooking oil until brown. Add the water, bay leaf and ginger and bring to the boil. Poach the fish steaks in this liquid until tender. When the fish is cooked remove from the liquor and place in a shallow dish. Add lemon juice and egg yolks to the cooking liquor. Heat gently, whisking all the time with a wire whisk, until the mixture thickens. Pour over the fish and leave to cool. Serve the next day.

1 onion, finely chopped
oil for frying
300ml/½pint water
1 bay leaf
½ teaspoon ground ginger
4 cod or hake steaks
juice 1 lemon
2 egg yolks, beaten

Smoked Fish Quiche

150g/5oz shortcrust pastry
225g/8oz smoked cod or
  haddock or kipper fillets
1 large onion, finely sliced
oil for frying
75g/3oz grated Cheddar cheese
3 eggs
150ml/¼pint milk
salt, pepper

Roll out pastry and use to line a 20cm/8in flan tin. Place fish in a pan with a little water and poach for 8-10 minutes. Remove from the cooking liquor, flake and leave to cool. Fry the onion in cooking oil until translucent. Arrange flaked fish and fried onion in the base of the flan and cover with cheese. Beat the eggs and milk together, season and pour into the flan. Bake at 190°C/375°F/Mark 5 for about 45 minutes until the top is golden brown and the quiche is set in the middle. Leave to cool for 20 minutes and then remove the flan case and place on a wire rack until completely cold.

Cod and Egg Mousse

225g/8oz cod fillet, skinned
300g/10oz canned condensed
  consommé
15g/½oz gelatine
2 tablespoons white wine
150ml/¼pint double cream
150ml/¼pint mayonnaise
  (page 66)
3 hard-boiled eggs, finely
  chopped
2 large gherkins or 1 small
  pickled cucumber, finely
  chopped
black pepper

Poach the fish in the undiluted consommé until tender and then blend until smooth. Mix the gelatine with wine and stand in a pan of hot water to dissolve. Whip the cream until fairly stiff and fold into the mayonnaise. Next add the fish and soup mixture, the eggs and gherkins and the gelatine. Season with black pepper to taste and pour into a wet mould. Place in the fridge to set. Turn out to serve.

Oriental Cod Salad

450g/1lb cooked cod or
  haddock, boned
1 lettuce
1 large onion, finely chopped
1 sweet apple, grated
25g/1oz butter
2 teaspoons curry powder
1 teaspoon ground cumin
80ml/3floz mayonnaise
  (page 66)
salt, pepper
2 tablespoons roasted almonds

Flake the fish and arrange on a bed of lettuce. Fry the onion and apple in butter with the spices. Cook for 5 minutes and leave to cool. Mix with mayonnaise and season to taste. Spoon this mixture over the fish and sprinkle with roasted almonds.

Spiced Fish Salad

Flake the fish coarsely. Place vinegar, garlic, Worcestershire sauce, cumin, tomato purée, water and seasoning in a pan and bring to the boil. Pour over the fish and leave to cool. Arrange the cabbage on a large plate. Drain the fish and arrange on the cabbage. Surround with sliced beetroot and cucumber and decorate with cress.

450g/1lb cooked white fish (cod, haddock, hake, huss or coley), skinned and boned
3 tablespoons vinegar
2 cloves garlic, crushed
1 teaspoon Worcestershire sauce
¼ teaspoon ground cumin
2 tablespoons tomato purée
150ml/¼pint water
salt, black pepper
½ small cabbage, finely sliced
2 cooked beetroots, peeled and sliced
¼ cucumber, sliced
1 box cress

Tomato Galantine of Cod

Soak gelatine in 2 tablespoons of the water and place the rest in a pan with tomatoes and onion. Bring to the boil and simmer until the onion is tender. Blend, mix with gelatine and season to taste. When the tomato jelly is just beginning to set, mix in the fish, parsley and cucumber. Pour into a wet mould and leave in the fridge to set. To serve, turn out and garnish with cucumber and hard-boiled egg and surround with lettuce.

15g/½oz gelatine
600ml/1pint water
225g/8oz tomatoes, skinned and sliced
1 onion, sliced
salt, pepper
600g/1¼lb cooked cod, flaked
1 tablespoon chopped parsley
7.5cm/3in length cucumber, diced

Garnish
2.5cm/1in length cucumber, thinly sliced
1 hard-boiled egg, sliced
lettuce leaves

Seafood Flan

Steam the sole. When it is cooked leave to cool and then cut into squares. Roll out the shortcrust pastry and use to line a 20cm/8in flan tin. Bake blind at 200°C/400°F/Mark 6 until golden brown and leave to cool. Arrange the pieces of sole and the prawns in the base of the flan and dot with gherkin slices. Place the mussels around the edge of the flan. Make up the aspic and pour over the flan. Place in the fridge to set.

1 lemon sole, filleted and skinned
150g/5oz shortcrust pastry
225g/8oz peeled prawns
6 cocktail gherkins, sliced
150g/5oz jar cooked mussels, drained
300ml/½pint aspic jelly

Celebration Fish Salad

450g/1lb cod steaks
1 lemon sole, filleted and
  skinned
1 small mackerel, cleaned
1 bay leaf
salt, pepper
100g/4oz peeled prawns
5 tablespoons mayonnaise
  (page 66)
2 tablespoons vinegar
2-3 teaspoons curry powder

Poach cod steaks, sole fillets and mackerel together in a little water with the bay leaf and seasoning. When the fish is cooked, leave it to cool and then remove any skin and bones. Place in bite-sized pieces on a large dish with the prawns. Mix mayonnaise, vinegar and curry powder and spoon all over the fish.

Pasta Prawn Salad

100g/4oz mixed pasta shapes
3 tablespoons salad oil
1 green/red pepper, deseeded
  and finely chopped
7.5cm/3in length cucumber,
  finely chopped
2 sticks celery, trimmed and
  finely chopped
450g/1lb peeled prawns
1 tablespoon lemon juice
1 tablespoon chopped parsley
¼ teaspoon dried oregano

Cook pasta in lightly salted water until tender, drain, cool and mix with salad oil. Mix the pepper, cucumber and celery with pasta, prawns, lemon juice and parsley. Turn into a bowl and sprinkle with oregano just before serving.

Salad Monte Cristo

2 dessert pears, peeled and
  diced
1 tablespoon mayonnaise
  (page 66)
1 bunch watercress, washed,
  picked over and coarsely
  chopped
225g/8oz peeled prawns
25g/1oz flaked almonds
½ teaspoon dried tarragon
salt, pepper
8 lettuce leaves

Mix the pears with the mayonnaise and add the watercress with the prawns, flaked almonds, tarragon and seasoning. Mix well and place in mounds on a bed of lettuce leaves. Sprinkle with a little more tarragon on top before serving.
Note: These quantities are sufficient for a small salad or starter. Use 3 pears and 350g/12oz prawns for a more substantial meal.

Seafood Salad

Mix the seafood with vinaigrette and arrange on a bed of lettuce leaves. Use the onion, tomatoes and cucumber to garnish the salad and serve with a bowl of mayonnaise.

750g/1½lb mixed cooked and shelled seafood (prawns, mussels, cockles, white crabmeat, shrimps and squid)
100ml/4floz vinaigrette **(page 68)**
lettuce leaves
1 small onion, finely sliced
2 tomatoes, quartered
2.5cm/1in length cucumber, sliced
mayonnaise **(page 66)**

Trout in Port Wine Jelly

Place port and water in a pan. Add the vegetables to the liquid with the bay leaf, seasoning and mixed spice. Bring to the boil and cook for 15-20 minutes. Next poach the trout in this liquor until tender. Lift out the fish and leave to cool. Dissolve the gelatine in a little water in a basin set over a pan of hot water. Strain the liquor from the fish and add the gelatine. When the fish are cold remove the heads, tails and skins and arrange the fish in a shallow dish. Colour the gelatine and cooking liquor with a little red food colouring and pour over the fish. Place in the fridge to set.

300ml/½pint port
300ml/½pint water
1 small carrot, sliced
1 small onion, sliced
1 stick celery, trimmed and sliced
1 bay leaf
salt, pepper, mixed spice
4 trout, cleaned
15g/½oz gelatine
red food colouring

Chaud-froid of Fish

If sole or plaice are being used, roll up the fillets before cooking. Cook the fish very carefully by steaming or poaching, taking care not to break it. Leave to cool. Arrange the rolled fillets or large flat fillet on a plate and coat with the chaud-froid. Serve garnished with tomatoes, gherkins and parsley.

450g/1lb sole or plaice fillets or 1 large haddock fillet
300ml/½pint chaud-froid **(page 67)**
2 tomatoes, halved
4 gherkins
sprigs parsley

Crab Tart

150g/5oz shortcrust pastry
½ green pepper, deseeded and
  finely chopped
100g/4oz dark crabmeat
2 tablespoons chopped chives
4 hard-boiled eggs
1 tablespoon mayonnaise
  (page 66)
salt, pepper
100g/4oz white crabmeat
1 tablespoon chopped parsley

Roll out the pastry and use to line a 20cm/8in flan tin. Bake blind at 200°C/400°F/Mark 6 until golden brown and crisp. Remove from the oven and leave to cool. Mix the green pepper with dark crabmeat and chives. Separate the egg yolks from the whites of 2 of the hard-boiled eggs and keep on one side. Finely chop the whites with the remaining 2 eggs and add to the crab mixture. Bind with mayonnaise and season to taste. Spread the mixture over the base of the pastry case. Next sprinkle the white crabmeat evenly over the top. Sieve the 2 egg yolks and decorate the top of the flan with chopped parsley and sieved yolk.

Anchovy Crabs

4 small cooked crabs
2 onions, finely chopped
150ml/¼ pint olive oil
4 tablespoons capers
4 tablespoons chopped parsley
4 tablespoons wine vinegar
2 teaspoons dry mustard
4 tablespoons chopped canned
  anchovy fillets
4 hard-boiled eggs

Remove crabmeat from the shells. Mix the onions with oil, capers, parsley, vinegar, mustard and anchovy fillets. Stir in first the dark meat and then the white meat and stuff back into the shells. Sieve the egg yolks and finely chop the egg whites and use to decorate the crabs.

Salmon Rice Cake

100g/4oz rice
2 hard-boiled eggs, finely
  chopped
200g/7oz canned salmon,
  drained and flaked
8 small spring onions, finely
  chopped
2 tablespoons chopped parsley
1 tablespoon mayonnaise
  (page 66)
salt, pepper
sprigs parsley

Cook rice in lightly salted water until tender. Wash, drain and leave to cool. Place all ingredients except parsley sprigs in a large bowl and mix well together. Grease a pudding basin, spoon the mixture into it and press well down. Chill for 2 hours. Turn out on to a serving dish and garnish with parsley sprigs.

Salmon and Egg Loaf

Combine the salmon and the butter and cream the mixture. Add the onion and celery and season to taste. Grease a 450g/1lb loaf tin and spoon a third of the mixture into it. Smooth the top. Lay half the eggs on top. Add 1 tablespoon each of mayonnaise and parsley. Next add another layer of salmon and repeat the layer of egg, mayonnaise and parsley. Finish off with the salmon. Place in the fridge and chill well. Turn out to serve and garnish with watercress.

400g/14oz canned salmon, drained and mashed
100g/4oz butter, softened
1 small onion, grated
4 sticks celery, trimmed and grated
salt, pepper
3 hard-boiled eggs, sliced
2 tablespoons mayonnaise (**page 66**)
2 tablespoons chopped parsley
sprigs watercress

Salmon Mousse

Melt the butter in a pan and stir in the flour. Gradually add the milk and the liquid from the can of salmon, stirring all the time. When the mixture thickens, cook for a further 2-3 minutes and remove from the heat. Finely mash the salmon and add to the sauce. Mix the gelatine with the white wine in a basin and stand in a pan of hot water until the gelatine dissolves. Add to the salmon mixture and fold in with the whipped cream. Spoon into a wet 18cm/7in ring mould and place in the fridge to set. Turn out to serve and decorate with thinly sliced cucumber and watercress.

25g/1oz butter
25g/1oz flour
300ml/½pint milk
200g/7oz canned salmon, drained and liquid reserved
15g/½oz gelatine
2 tablespoons white wine
150ml/¼pint whipping cream, stiffly whipped
5cm/2in length cucumber, thinly sliced
sprigs watercress

Salmon in White Wine Jelly

Place the salmon steaks in cold dry white wine with the bay leaf and peppercorns. Bring to the boil and boil for 1 minute. Turn off the heat and leave to cool. Reserve the liquor, remove the steaks and skin. Place on a large serving dish. Decorate the steaks with hard-boiled egg, cucumber, gherkin and olive slices. Strain the liquor the fish was cooked in and mix a little of it with the gelatine. Place over a pan of hot water to dissolve and mix with the remaining stock. Just before it begins to set use to coat the decorated fish. Place in the fridge to set. Keep any remaining jelly and chop to place round the fish steaks just before serving.

4 salmon steaks
½ bottle dry white wine
1 bay leaf
3 peppercorns
1 hard-boiled egg, sliced
2.5cm/1in length cucumber, sliced
4 gherkins, sliced
4 stuffed olives, sliced
15g/½oz gelatine

8 Canapés, Savouries and Suppers

Canapés

Sardine Bites

125g/4½oz canned sardines in
    tomato sauce
75g/3oz cream cheese
salt, pepper
6 slices buttered bread
2 eggs, beaten
oil for frying

Empty the contents of the can of sardines into a basin and mash well with cream cheese until very smooth. Season to taste. Spread on to 3 slices of bread and top with remaining slices. Cut off the crusts and cut each sandwich into 4 triangles. Dip each triangle in beaten egg and fry quickly on both sides in cooking oil. Serve at once.

Clarence Canapés

4 slices bread
oil for deep frying
8-12 rashers streaky bacon
100g/4oz mushrooms, finely
    chopped
1 slice cooked ham, finely
    chopped
anchovy butter (**page 69**)
chopped parsley

Cut each slice of bread into 2 or 3 fancy shapes with pastry cutters and deep fry in oil until golden brown. Drain and leave to cool. Grill the streaky bacon. Fry the mushrooms gently in a little cooking oil until they are soft; leave to cool. Mix the ham with the mushrooms and bind with anchovy butter. Spread this mixture along the grilled bacon and roll up. Place each bacon roll on a piece of fried bread and decorate with chopped parsley.

Anchovy and Olive Canapés

50g/2oz canned anchovy fillets,
    soaked and drained
12 stuffed olives
100g/4oz butter, softened
4 slices toast, crusts removed

Mince the anchovy fillets with 10 of the stuffed olives. Add the softened butter and spread the toast with this canapé mixture. Cut each slice into triangles. Thinly slice the remaining olives and use to decorate the canapés.

146

Egg and Anchovy Canapés

Cut 4 round shapes the same size as a slice of egg out of each slice of bread and deep fry in cooking oil until golden brown. Drain and leave to cool. Place a round of egg on each croûton. Top with a stuffed olive with an anchovy wrapped round it.

4 slices bread
oil for deep frying
2 hard-boiled eggs, sliced
16 stuffed olives
16 canned anchovy fillets, soaked and drained

Brisling Canapés

Toast the slices of bread and remove crusts. Cut into 4 or 5 strips depending on the number of fish in the can. Place one smoked brisling on each strip. Place an olive slice on each brisling. Arrange the brisling fingers on a plate and top with parsley sprigs.

4 slices small brown tin loaf
100g/4oz canned smoked brisling in tomato sauce, drained
4 stuffed olives, sliced
sprigs parsley

Prunes Stuffed with Mussels and Cream Cheese

Bring the prunes to the boil in the water they were soaked in and simmer until just tender. Drain and leave to cool. Soften the cream cheese with single cream or milk and season to taste. When the prunes are cold remove stones and stuff with cream cheese and a single mussel. Serve with cocktail sticks.

16 prunes, soaked in cold water overnight
75g/3oz cream cheese
1 tablespoon single cream or milk
salt, pepper
16 canned mussels

Smoked Gems

Melt the butter in a pan and add the flour. Stir well and gradually add the milk. Bring to the boil, stirring all the time. Continue cooking for 2-3 minutes and then remove from the heat. Poach smoked haddock in a little water. When cooked, drain, skin and flake the fish. Leave to cool. Mix the cheese into the sauce before it cools completely. Add the egg yolk and fork in the flaked fish. Season to taste. Place the mixture in the fridge for 2-3 hours. Shape the mixture into balls, dip in beaten egg and then roll in breadcrumbs. Quickly deep fry in hot oil until golden. Do not leave in the hot fat for too long or the centres will begin to run. Drain and serve at once.

50g/2oz butter
50g/2oz flour
250ml/8floz milk
100g/4oz smoked haddock or cod
175g/6oz Camembert or Brie, finely diced
1 egg yolk
salt, pepper
1 egg, beaten
dry breadcrumbs
oil for deep frying

Samosas

Pastry
100g/4oz flour
salt
25g/1oz butter
2-3 tablespoons water
oil for deep frying

Filling
225g/8oz potatoes
100g/4oz huss
25g/1oz butter
1 tablespoon ground cumin
½ teaspoon ground ginger
½ teaspoon chilli powder
black pepper
2 tablespoons frozen peas

To make the filling, cook the potatoes in their skins in lightly salted water until tender. Steam the huss on a plate on top of the potatoes. Leave to cool and then peel and dice potatoes and dice the fish. Melt butter in a frying pan with the spices and sauté the potatoes, fish and peas in this until the potatoes and fish are lightly browned.

Meanwhile make pastry by mixing flour and salt and rubbing in the butter until the mixture resembles fine breadcrumbs. Bind with water and knead until the dough is firm and pliable. Roll the pastry out thinly and cut into 8 squares.

Place a little of the filling on each square and fold over in a triangular shape. Damp the edges and pinch together. Heat the oil and when it is really hot fry the samosas until golden brown. Drain on kitchen paper and serve at once.

Assorted Pin Wheels

200g/7oz cream cheese
2 tablespoons single cream
1-2 teaspoons anchovy essence
salt, pepper
25g/1oz minced smoked
  salmon bits
25g/1oz cod roe
6 slices fresh bread

Mix cream cheese with single cream to give a smooth creamy consistency. Divide the mixture in half and mix one half with anchovy essence and season to taste. Divide the remaining half again, mixing one part with minced smoked salmon and the other with cod roe. Season both to taste and add a little more cream if the mixtures seem to be too thick. Spread 2 slices of bread with each mixture. Remove the crusts and roll up lengthways. Slice into 5 pin wheels per slice.

Smoked Haddock Profiteroles

Profiteroles
25g/1oz butter
150ml/¼pint water
50g/2oz flour
salt
1 egg
1 egg yolk

Filling
100g/4oz smoked haddock
milk
salt, pepper
100g/4oz cream cheese

Heat butter and water in a pan and when it boils remove from the heat. Stir in the flour and salt and mix well. Add the egg and egg yolk one at a time beating well between each addition. Spoon 16-20 small mounds on to a greased baking tray. Bake at 200°C/400°F/Mark 6 for about 20 minutes until the outside is golden brown and crisp and the inside is dry. Slit each profiterole and place on a wire rack to cool.

To make the filling, poach the haddock in a little seasoned milk. When it is cooked, remove from the cooking liquor, mash thoroughly with a fork and leave to cool. Mix with cream cheese, adding a little of the cooking liquor if the mixture is too thick. Use to fill the profiteroles.

Egg and Mock Caviar Cocktail Cups

Use a pastry cutter to cut bread into 12 rounds large enough to
fit into deep bun trays. Butter each round with softened butter
and press into the cups of the bun tray. Bake at 180°C/
350°F/Mark 4 for 25-30 minutes until golden brown. Remove
from the tray and place on a wire rack to cool. Heat butter and
milk in a pan and add the eggs. Cook over a low heat, stirring all
the time. Do not allow the eggs to overcook. Season to taste and
leave to cool. Fill bread cups with cold scrambled egg and top
with lumpfish roe.

12 small slices white bread
50g/2oz butter, softened
15g/½oz butter
2 tablespoons milk
3 eggs, beaten
salt, pepper
50g/2oz jar lumpfish roe

Smoked Eel and Pimento Canapés

Mince the eel with the pimentos. Mix with the butter and season
to taste with black pepper and lemon juice. Fry the bread in oil,
drain and leave to cool. Spread the eel and pimento mixture on
the bread and cut each slice into 8 small squares or triangles.

100g/4oz smoked eel, skinned
  and boned
100g/4oz canned or bottled
  pimentos
25g/1oz butter, softened
black pepper
lemon juice
2 slices bread
oil for frying

Shrimp Prunes

Gently poach the prunes in the water they were soaked in. Mix
the shrimps with mayonnaise and season to taste. When the
prunes are tender, drain and leave to cool. Remove the stones
and stuff each prune with a little of the shrimp mixture.

16 prunes, soaked in cold
  water overnight
50g/2oz peeled shrimps or
  prawns, finely chopped
1 tablespoon mayonnaise
  (page 66)
salt, pepper

Egg and Shrimp Tartlets

Roll out pastry and use to line 12-18 small tartlet tins. Prick the
bases with a fork. Fill with foil and dry beans and bake blind at
200°C/400°F/Mark 6 for about 10 minutes. Remove the foil and
beans and continue cooking until golden in colour. Remove from
tins and place on a wire rack to cool.

   To make the filling, mix eggs, shrimps or prawns and mayonnaise and season to taste. Spoon into the tartlets and top with
chopped parsley.

175g/6oz shortcrust pastry

Filling
4 hard-boiled eggs, chopped
200g/7oz canned shrimps or
  prawns, drained
2 tablespoons mayonnaise
  (page 66)
salt, pepper
chopped parsley

Chinese Shrimp Toast

225g/8oz peeled shrimps or
  prawns, finely minced
6 spring onions, finely minced
1 small egg, beaten
½ teaspoon ground ginger
1 teaspoon sugar
1 tablespoon cornflour
salt, pepper
4 slices bread, crusts removed
2 tablespoons sesame seeds
oil for frying

Mix the shrimps or prawns and spring onions with the egg. Add ginger, sugar, cornflour and seasoning. Spread each slice of bread with the shrimp mixture and sprinkle with sesame seeds. Press these well into the top. Heat the cooking oil in a frying pan. Fry the slices of shrimp toast in oil, bread side down, until the bread turns golden brown. Turn over and fry the other side until it, too, turns golden brown. Remove from the fat and drain on kitchen paper. Cut into fingers and serve at once.

Moscow Canapés

4 slices bread
oil for deep frying
50g/2oz caviar or lumpfish
  roe
2 tablespoons mayonnaise
  (page 66)
chopped parsley
cayenne

Cut 3 fancy shapes from each piece of bread with pastry cutters. Deep fry in cooking oil until golden brown. Leave to cool. Spread each base with caviar or lumpfish roe and top with mayonnaise. Sprinkle alternate canapés with chopped parsley or cayenne pepper.

Smoked Salmon Cornets

225g/8oz smoked salmon

Filling 1
2 eggs
15g/½oz butter
1 tablespoon milk
½ teaspoon dried tarragon
salt, pepper

Filling 2
1 portion smoked mackerel pâté
  (page 79)
1 tablespoon double cream

Garnish
parsley
lemon wedges

Scramble the eggs with the butter and milk. Cook to a creamy consistency and remove from the heat. Do not overcook as the eggs will go hard and lumpy. Leave to cool and mix with tarragon and season to taste. Mix the mackerel pâté with cream to a smooth consistency. Cut the smoked salmon into 16 triangles and place a teaspoonful of egg filling in the centre of 8 of them and a teaspoonful of creamed pâté in the centre of the other 8. Roll up to make 16 cornets. Garnish with parsley and lemon wedges.

Savouries

Cheese and Sardine Fingers

Mash the contents of the can of sardines with a fork and spread over the toast. Sprinkle with chervil or parsley. Cut the slices of cheese to fit the toast and place on top. Place under a hot grill and cook until the cheese is brown and bubbling. Cut each slice into 3 fingers before serving.

125g/4½oz canned sardines in tomato sauce
4 slices toast, crusts removed
1 teaspoon chopped chervil or parsley
4 slices cheese

Scotch Woodcock

Beat the eggs and scramble with the butter and milk. Season to taste. Butter the toast and spread the scrambled eggs on top. Decorate with a lattice design of anchovy fillets.

3 eggs
15g/½oz butter
2 tablespoons milk
salt, pepper
4 slices toast
50g/2oz canned anchovy fillets, soaked and drained

Savoury à l'Indienne

Cut the toast or fried bread in half. Butter the toast. Scramble the eggs with the butter and milk and stir in anchovy essence, capers and gherkins. Season to taste and spread on the toast or fried bread slices. Decorate with anchovy fillets.

4 slices toast or fried bread, crusts removed
4 eggs
15g/½oz butter
2 tablespoons milk
1 tablespoon anchovy essence
1 tablespoon capers
2 gherkins, chopped
salt, pepper
8 canned anchovy fillets, soaked and drained

Smoked Haddock Savoury

Cut the bread slices in half. Deep fry each piece until golden brown. Steam the smoked haddock, skin and flake. Mix cornflour with cream and place in a pan with flaked fish. Heat through stirring all the time. When the mixture thickens season to taste and spread on the fried bread slices. Sprinkle the gherkins on the top.

4 slices bread, crusts removed
oil for deep frying
175g/6oz smoked haddock
½ teaspoon cornflour
2 tablespoons double cream
salt, pepper
4 gherkins, finely chopped

Bacon and Smoked Mussel Rolls

small strips streaky bacon
100g/4oz canned smoked
   mussels, drained
fried bread croûtons

Cut sufficient strips of bacon to wrap round each mussel. Secure with a cocktail stick and place under a hot grill until the bacon is crisp. Serve on croûtons.

Soft Roe Savoury

soft roes from 8 herrings (about
   225g/8oz), rinsed
300ml/½pint milk and water
4 slices toast
2 tablespoons cornflour
1 teaspoon French mustard
salt, pepper, cayenne
chopped parsley

Poach the roes in milk and water until tender. Place 4 roes on each slice of toast and keep hot. Mix the cornflour to a smooth paste with a little cold water and add the boiled milk and water from the roes. Bring to the boil, stirring all the time. Add mustard, salt, pepper and a pinch of cayenne. Cook for 3-4 minutes and pour over the roes. Top with a little chopped parsley.

Soft Roes with Mushrooms

soft roes from 4 herrings (about
   100g/4oz), rinsed
150ml/¼pint milk and water
salt, pepper
8 field mushrooms
butter
4 slices toast
chopped parsley

Poach the roes in milk and water. Drain and keep hot. Season the mushrooms and dot with butter. Grill until tender. Arrange the mushrooms on each piece of toast with a soft roe on either side. Top with a little chopped parsley.

Kipper Scramble

2 eggs
15g/½oz butter
1 tablespoon milk
salt, pepper
100g/4oz cooked kipper fillets,
   flaked
4 small slices toast
chopped parsley

Beat the eggs and scramble with the butter and milk. Season and add the flaked fish. Butter the toast and spread the egg and kipper mixture on the top. Garnish with a little chopped parsley.

Grilled Kipper Squares

Arrange the kipper fillets on the slices of toast. Mix bread-crumbs, parsley and cheese and sprinkle over the kipper fillets. Next sprinkle with lemon juice and dot with butter. Place under a hot grill for about 3-4 minutes.

4 cooked kipper fillets
4 slices toast
25g/1oz breadcrumbs
1 tablespoon chopped parsley
1 tablespoon grated Parmesan
  cheese
juice 1 lemon
butter

Curried Shrimps on Toast

Toast the bread and remove the crusts. Make the velouté sauce and add curry powder to taste. Cook for 5 minutes. Add the shrimps or prawns to the sauce. Spoon on to the toast and top with cheese. Place under a hot grill until the cheese is crisp and golden.

4 slices bread
150ml/¼pint velouté sauce
  (page 60)
½-1 teaspoon curry powder
100g/4oz peeled shrimps or
  prawns, chopped
2 tablespoons grated cheese

Angels on Horseback

Season bacon strips with paprika and sprinkle with parsley and lemon juice. Lay an oyster on each piece and roll up. Secure with a cocktail stick. Place under a hot grill until the bacon is crisp. Remove cocktail sticks and serve on toast.

12 small strips streaky bacon
paprika
1 teaspoon chopped parsley
lemon juice
12 oysters opened
4 slices toast

Oysters Florentine

Fry the bread in cooking oil until golden on both sides. Drain, cut into 2 and leave to cool. Heat the oysters through in a double steamer. Place spinach purée in a pan and heat through. Mix with cream and place a little of the mixture on each piece of fried bread. Place 2 warm oysters on each and press into the spinach. Sprinkle with cayenne pepper and serve at once.

4 slices bread, crusts removed
oil for frying
16 oysters, opened
100g/4oz frozen spinach purée,
  thawed
1 tablespoon cream
cayenne

Suppers

Tagliatelli with Anchovy Parmesan Sauce

225g/8oz tagliatelli
225g/8oz mushrooms, sliced
50g/2oz butter
2 teaspoons anchovy essence
300ml/½pint double cream
salt, pepper
50g/2oz grated Parmesan
   cheese
4 canned anchovy fillets,
   drained and chopped

Cook tagliatelli in lightly salted water until tender. Sauté mushrooms in butter until tender. Drain the pasta and add the mushrooms and butter. Toss in the pan, add anchovy essence and double cream and season to taste. Serve sprinkled with Parmesan cheese and chopped anchovy fillets.

Sardines Bonne Femme

250g/9oz canned sardines in
   oil, drained
1 onion, finely chopped
4 tomatoes, skinned and
   quartered
50g/2oz breadcrumbs
1 tablespoon grated Parmesan
   cheese
butter

Grease a casserole dish and arrange the sardines in the base of it. Sprinkle the onion over the top. Arrange the tomatoes round the edge of the dish. Sprinkle the centre with breadcrumbs and Parmesan and dot with butter. Bake at 190°C/375°F/Mark 5 for 20 minutes. If the top is not sufficiently browned finish off under the grill.

Quick Mackerel Casserole

425g/15oz canned mackerel,
   drained
300g/10oz canned condensed
   asparagus, tomato or
   mushroom soup
1 teaspoon dried marjoram
black pepper
50g/2oz grated cheese
50g/2oz breadcrumbs

Flake the mackerel coarsely with a fork. Turn into a casserole dish and spoon the condensed soup over the top. Sprinkle with marjoram and black pepper. Mix the cheese and breadcrumbs and use to cover the dish. Bake at 200°C/400°F/Mark 6 for 40 minutes. If necessary brown the top under the grill.

Mackerel and Tomato Pie

Parboil potatoes and drain well. Fry the onions in oil until transparent. Slice potatoes and mix with onions. Place half this mixture in the base of a casserole dish. Flake the mackerel in the can and pour contents over the potato and onion mixture. Add tomatoes, retaining the juice. Cover with the remaining potato and onion mixture. Pour over the juice from the can of tomatoes. Season and sprinkle with fennel seed and bake at 220°C/425°F/Mark 7 for 20-30 minutes.

1kg/2lb potatoes
2 onions, sliced
oil for frying
425g/15oz canned mackerel in
   tomato sauce
225g/8oz canned tomatoes
salt, pepper
¼ teaspoon fennel seed

Pilchard Quiche

Roll out pastry and use to line an 18cm/7in flan tin. Bake blind at 190°C/375°F/Mark 5 for 10 minutes. Drain the can of pilchards and mix the juice with the cottage cheese, yogurt, milk and eggs and beat well. Season to taste. Remove flan case from oven and flake the pilchards over the base. Pour on the egg mixture and return to the oven for a further 45 minutes.

150g/5oz shortcrust pastry
150g/5oz canned pilchards in
   tomato sauce
100g/4oz cottage cheese
1 tablespoon yogurt
1 tablespoon milk
2 eggs
salt, pepper

Dabs Davida

Roll the dabs in seasoned flour and fry in 25g/1oz butter for about 3-4 minutes on each side. Meanwhile melt remaining butter in another pan and fry the breadcrumbs until golden. When the fish are cooked place on a large serving plate and sprinkle with parsley and lemon juice. Scatter the fried breadcrumbs over the top.

4 dabs, small flounders or
   plaice, cleaned
4 tablespoons seasoned flour
75g/3oz butter
50g/2oz breadcrumbs
2 tablespoons chopped parsley
juice 1 lemon

Quick Creamed Fish

Pour the soup, lemon juice and milk into a pan and heat through, stirring from time to time. Add peas, pimentos and fish and season with black pepper to taste. Fry the bread in butter until crisp and golden on both sides. Cut into small squares. When the fish mixture is really hot spoon into individual dishes and top with fried bread squares.

300g/10oz canned condensed
   cream of celery soup
1 tablespoon lemon juice
3 tablespoons milk
4 tablespoons cooked peas
1 tablespoon chopped canned
   red pimentos
350g/12oz cooked fish (coley,
   pollack or whiting), flaked
black pepper
2 slices bread
butter

Fish Burgers

450g/1lb coley
300ml/½pint milk
salt, pepper
1 bay leaf
1 large onion, finely chopped
100g/4oz mushrooms, finely
    chopped
oil for frying
50g/2oz flour
175g/6oz breadcrumbs
1 teaspoon dried marjoram
1 egg, beaten

Poach coley in milk with salt and pepper and bay leaf. Drain and flake the fish; reserve the liquor. Gently fry the onion and mushrooms in oil until tender. Add flour, stir well and add cooking liquor from coley. Bring to the boil, stirring all the time, cook for a few minutes and then add fish, half the breadcrumbs and the marjoram. Season to taste and shape into burgers. Dip in beaten egg and coat with remaining breadcrumbs. Fry on each side until golden brown.

Parsley and Tarragon Fish Cakes

350g/12oz cooked white fish
    (huss, coley or pollack),
    flaked
450g/1lb cooked mashed potato
50g/2oz fresh breadcrumbs
3 tablespoons double cream
2 teaspoons anchovy essence
3 tablespoons chopped parsley
1 teaspoon dried tarragon
salt, pepper
dry breadcrumbs
oil for frying

Mash the fish with a fork. Add the mashed potato, fresh breadcrumbs, cream, anchovy essence, herbs and seasonings. Beat to a smooth paste. Shape into flat cakes and coat with dry breadcrumbs. Fry in oil on each side until golden brown in colour.

Creole Cakes

450g/1lb cooked white fish
    (huss, coley, pollack or
    whiting), flaked
25g/1oz butter
175g/6oz wholemeal
    breadcrumbs
1 onion, grated
1 clove garlic, crushed
1 tablespoon chopped parsley
½ teaspoon dried oregano
salt, pepper
1 egg, beaten
dry breadcrumbs
oil for frying

Mash the fish with a fork. Melt the butter in a pan and add to the fish with the wholemeal breadcrumbs, onion, garlic, herbs and seasoning. Mix thoroughly and shape into small flat cakes. Coat with egg and then with dry breadcrumbs and fry in oil on each side until golden brown.

Devilled Whiting Bake

Poach whiting in a little milk with sliced onion until tender. Drain and skin the fish and mix with strained onion. Mix potatoes with remaining ingredients and add the fish mixture. Beat well. Grease a casserole dish and turn the mixture into it. Bake at 190°C/375°F/Mark 5 for 40 minutes until set in the centre and golden brown on top.

750g/1½lb whiting fillets
milk
1 onion, sliced
225g/8oz potatoes, grated
1 tablespoon tomato purée
1 teaspoon prepared mustard
1 teaspoon Worcestershire
  sauce
4 eggs
salt, pepper

Spanish Whiting

Mix the onion, orange rind, half the orange juice, breadcrumbs, raisins, melted butter, herbs and seasoning in a bowl. Spread this mixture over the fillets and roll up. Secure with cocktail sticks. Grease an ovenproof dish and place the fillets in it. Pour the remaining orange juice over the fish, cover and bake at 190°C/375°F/Mark 5 for 20 minutes.

8 whiting fillets

Stuffing
1 small onion, finely chopped
grated rind and juice 2 oranges
100g/4oz breadcrumbs
75g/3oz raisins
25g/1oz butter, melted
½ teaspoon dried mixed herbs
salt, pepper

Huss Parmesan

Season the huss with salt and pepper. Mix the breadcrumbs and Parmesan. Coat the chunks of fish in flour, dip in egg and then press the breadcrumb and cheese mixture all over the outside. Deep fry in hot oil for 2-3 minutes until golden brown. Serve garnished with lemon wedges and with tartar sauce (**page 68**).

225g/8oz huss, cut into chunks
salt, pepper
50g/2oz breadcrumbs
25g/1oz grated Parmesan
  cheese
2 tablespoons flour
1 egg, beaten
oil for deep frying
lemon wedges

Scalloped Cod Roe

Simmer the cod roe in salted water for 10 minutes. Drain and mash with a fork. Mix with melted butter. Add the spring onions, hard-boiled egg and breadcrumbs. Season to taste and spoon into scallop shells. Dot with butter and bake at 190°C/375°F/Mark 5 for 20 minutes.

450g/1lb cod roe
50g/2oz butter, melted
4 spring onions, finely chopped
1 hard-boiled egg, finely
  chopped
50g/2oz breadcrumbs
salt, pepper
butter

Puff Pancakes

Pancakes
100g/4oz flour
salt
2 eggs, separated
300ml/½pint milk
oil for frying

Filling
450g/1lb tomatoes, coarsely
  chopped
½ teaspoon dried oregano
¼ teaspoon celery salt
350g/12oz huss, coley or
  pollack
1 teaspoon cornflour
150ml/¼pint soured cream

Sift flour and salt into a basin and add the egg yolks and half the milk. Beat well with a fork and then add remaining milk and leave to stand for 30 minutes. Whisk the egg whites until really stiff and fold into the batter. Use the batter to make 4 thick pancakes and keep warm.

Place the tomatoes in a pan with oregano and celery salt. Bring to the boil and simmer for 10 minutes. Liquidise and return to the pan. Cut the fish into very small pieces and cook in the tomato sauce for 10 minutes. Thicken with cornflour. Remove from the heat and add sufficient soured cream to give a thick creamy consistency. Heat through but do not boil. Divide the filling between the 4 pancakes. Fold the pancakes over once, pour remaining soured cream over the top and serve at once.

Florentine Toast

225g/8oz frozen spinach purée
4 eggs
15g/½oz butter
2 tablespoons milk
salt, pepper
100g/4oz smoked eel, skinned,
  boned and sliced
4 slices toast
2 tablespoons double cream
nutmeg

Thaw frozen spinach as directed on the packet. Beat the eggs and scramble with the butter and milk. Season to taste. Warm the smoked eel in a double steamer and arrange along 2 sides of each slice of toast. Fill the centre with scrambled eggs. Mix the cream into the spinach and spoon over the eggs and eel. Top with a little nutmeg.

Pasta Paesana

200g/7oz canned tuna
2 tablespoons oil
2 onions, finely chopped
3 cloves garlic, finely chopped
1 tablespoon dried basil
1 teaspoon dried oregano
6 canned anchovy fillets,
  drained and chopped
225g/8oz canned tomatoes
salt, pepper
225g/8oz spaghetti

Drain the oil from the tuna into a frying pan, add the cooking oil and fry the onions and garlic. Add the herbs and cook for 5 minutes. Add the anchovies. Next pour in the contents of the can of tomatoes, bring to the boil and cook for a further 10 minutes. Flake the tuna and add to the pan with seasoning to taste. Heat through. Meanwhile cook the spaghetti in lightly salted boiling water until just tender. Drain and serve with the tuna sauce over the top.

Bean and Tuna Pancakes

Sift flour and salt into a basin and add the egg and half the milk. Beat well with a fork and then add remaining milk and leave to stand for 30 minutes. Use this batter to make 8 pancakes allowing a little over 3 tablespoonfuls for each. Place the pancakes on a plate and keep warm.

Chop the beans into 5mm/¼in lengths and cook in lightly salted water until tender. Drain and set aside. Make a sauce by melting the butter in a saucepan and adding the flour. Gradually stir in the milk and continue cooking, stirring all the time, until the mixture thickens. Cook for a further 3-4 minutes and then add the beans, tuna and herbs and season to taste. Fill the pancakes and serve at once.

Pancakes
100g/4oz flour
salt
1 egg
300ml/½pint milk
oil for frying

Filling
350g/12oz green beans (French or runner), topped, tailed and strings removed
25g/1oz butter
25g/1oz flour
450ml/16floz milk
200g/7oz canned tuna, drained and flaked
¼ teaspoon dried mixed herbs
salt, pepper

Tuna Lasagne

Cook lasagne in lightly salted water until tender. Place tuna and tomatoes in a pan and add the onion, oregano, tomato purée and seasoning. Bring to the boil and sprinkle on the flour, stir and continue cooking gently for 10 minutes.

Melt butter in a pan and add the flour. Stir and gradually add the milk. Bring to the boil, stirring all the time. Add half the cheese and season to taste. Layer lasagne, tuna sauce and cheese sauce in a shallow earthenware dish. Sprinkle with remaining cheese and bake at 200°C/400°F/Mark 6 until brown on top.

8 pieces lasagne

Tuna sauce
200g/7oz canned tuna, drained
225g/8oz canned tomatoes
1 onion, finely chopped
½ teaspoon dried oregano
1 tablespoon tomato purée
salt, pepper
1 tablespoon flour

Cheese sauce
50g/2oz butter
50g/2oz flour
600ml/1pint milk
50g/2oz grated Parmesan cheese
salt, pepper

Smoked Haddock Omelette

Poach haddock in a little milk and water until cooked. Remove skin and bone and flake. Return the fish to the pan with 2 tablespoons of the cooking liquor, the Parmesan cheese and cream and toss quickly over the heat. Place on one side but keep warm. Season the eggs to taste. Make 1 large or 4 individual omelettes and fill with haddock mixture. Sprinkle with extra black pepper, fold over and serve.

225g/8oz smoked haddock
milk and water
2 tablespoons grated Parmesan cheese
2 tablespoons double cream
salt, pepper
8 eggs, beaten

Stuffed Baked Potatoes

4 large potatoes
100g/4oz mushrooms, sliced
juice 1 lemon
225g/8oz smoked haddock or
    cod
25g/1oz butter
salt, pepper
50g/2oz grated cheese
1 tomato, sliced

Bake the potatoes in their jackets. Simmer the mushrooms in lemon juice for 5 minutes. Drain and set aside. Poach the fish in a little water. When the fish is cooked remove any skin and bones and flake. When the potatoes are cooked cut in half and scoop out the pulp. Mash with butter. Add mushrooms and fish and season to taste. Stuff this mixture back into the empty jackets. Sprinkle with cheese and arrange a slice of tomato on top of each half. Finish off under the grill.

Smoked Haddock and Green Pea Quiche

150g/5oz shortcrust pastry
100g/4oz smoked haddock
milk
175g/6oz frozen peas
75g/3oz grated Cheddar cheese
3 eggs, beaten
150ml/¼pint single cream
salt, pepper

Roll out pastry and use to line an 18cm/7in flan tin. Place smoked haddock in a pan with a little milk and poach for 10 minutes until cooked. Remove fish from the milk, flake and leave to cool; reserve the liquor. Thaw peas for 2 minutes in boiling water and drain. Place haddock and peas in the base of the flan. Cover with cheese. Beat eggs with cream and the fish liquor. Season and pour over the flan. Bake at 190°C/375°F/Mark 5 for about 45 minutes until the top is golden brown and the quiche is set in the centre.

Smoky Pancakes

Pancakes
100g/4oz flour
salt
1 egg
300ml/½pint milk
oil for frying

Filling
350g/12oz frozen smoked
    haddock or kipper fillets with
    butter
175g/6oz cream cheese
80ml/3floz double cream
4 tablespoons finely chopped
    parsley
salt, pepper

Sift flour and salt into a basin and add the egg and half the milk. Beat well with a fork and then add remaining milk and leave to stand for 30 minutes. Use this batter to make 8 pancakes, allowing a little over 3 tablespoonfuls for each. Place the pancakes on a plate and keep warm.

Cook haddock or kippers as directed on the packet. When cooked, remove any skin and bone and flake with the cooking juices. Mix cream cheese and double cream to a smooth paste and then mix in the fish. Add parsley and season to taste. Transfer to a pan and gently warm through. Do not allow the mixture to boil. When it is really hot use to fill the pancakes.

Smoked Fish Cakes

Cook smoked haddock fillets as directed on the packet. Cook potatoes in lightly salted water until tender. Drain and mash potatoes and mix with the liquid from the fish. Flake the fish with a fork, removing any bones, and add to the potato mixture. Add breadcrumbs, anchovy essence and chives and season to taste. Shape the mixture into 8 flat cakes. Coat each cake with beaten egg and then with dry breadcrumbs. Fry in oil on each side until golden brown.

350g/12oz frozen smoked
  haddock fillets with butter
350g/12oz potatoes
50g/2oz breadcrumbs
1 teaspoon anchovy essence
1 tablespoon chopped chives
salt, pepper
1 egg, beaten
dry breadcrumbs
oil for frying

Fish Mumble

Poach haddock in a little milk and water until cooked. Remove skin and bone and flake. Boil potatoes in their skins in lightly salted water and, when cooked, peel and chop them. Melt the butter in a shallow pan and add fish, potatoes, parsley, garlic and seasoning. Pour the eggs over the potatoes and fish. Stir into the mixture until cooked. Serve sprinkled with a little more parsley.

450g/1lb smoked haddock or
  cod
milk and water
450g/1lb potatoes
25g/1oz butter
2 tablespoons chopped parsley
1 clove garlic, crushed
salt, pepper
2 eggs, beaten

Windsor Pie

Grease a pie dish and place the fish in the base of it. Sprinkle with potted shrimps, retaining any large chunks of shrimp butter. Sauté the mushrooms in butter and shrimp butter. Place mushrooms on top of the fish. Mix cornflour with sherry and pour into the pan the mushrooms have been cooked in. Add mixed fish stock and milk and bring to the boil, stirring all the time. Season to taste and pour over the fish. Roll out the pastry and top the pie with this. Fork the edges and prick the centre and bake at 220°C/425°F/Mark 7 for 20 minutes.

450g/1lb cooked white fish
  (haddock, hake, cod or
  coley), flaked
1 carton potted shrimps
100g/4oz mushrooms, sliced
25g/1oz butter
1 tablespoon cornflour
2 tablespoons sherry
150ml/¼pint fish stock and
  milk
salt, pepper
100g/4oz shortcrust pastry

Fish Crumble

750g/1½lb fish fillets (haddock, coley, huss or pollack), skinned
450g/1lb leeks, trimmed and sliced
225g/8oz canned tomatoes
salt, pepper
50g/2oz butter
50g/2oz flour
50g/2oz grated cheese

Remove any bones from the fish fillets and cut into chunks. Mix the leeks with the fish and place this mixture in the base of an ovenproof dish. Pour the tomatoes over the top and add seasoning. Rub the butter into the flour until the mixture resembles fine breadcrumbs, then mix in the cheese. Sprinkle the crumble topping over the fish and bake at 190°C/375°F/Mark 5 for 30-35 minutes.

Bulgarian Fish Supper

450g/1lb potatoes, chopped
2 onions, chopped
1 large green pepper, deseeded and coarsely chopped
4 tomatoes, skinned and coarsely chopped
4 tablespoons rice
salt, pepper
450g/1lb white fish (cod, coley or haddock)

Mix all the vegetables together in a large casserole dish. Add rice and seasoning and mix again. Cover and bake at 190°C/375°F/Mark 5 for 30 minutes. Skin and bone the fish, if necessary, and cut into chunks. Stir into the casserole mixture. Replace the lid and continue cooking for a further 30 minutes. Serve with tomato sauce (**page 66**) if desired.

Scandinavian Fish Pasty

225g/8oz shortcrust pastry
225g/8oz cooked white fish (cod, haddock, coley or pollack), flaked
100g/4oz cooked rice
2 shallots or spring onions, finely chopped
2 large mushrooms, finely chopped
1 tablespoon chopped parsley
salt, pepper
2 hard-boiled eggs, sliced

Roll out pastry into a 25cm/10in square. Mix the fish with the rice. Mix the shallots, mushrooms and parsley with fish and rice. Season to taste. Place half the mixture in the centre of the pastry. Arrange the eggs on top. Cover with remaining fish mixture. Fold the pastry over the top and seal. Also seal the ends. Make 3-4 slashes across the top of the pastry and place on a greased baking tray. Bake at 200°C/400°F/Mark 6 for 25-30 minutes until the pastry is lightly browned. Serve with tomato sauce (**page 66**).

Mexican Fish Pie

Grease a casserole dish and place the cod steaks in the base of it. Mix the tomatoes and green pepper with salt and pepper and chilli powder to taste. Place the onions on top of the cod. Sprinkle on the rice and top with tomato chilli mixture. Cover with a lid and bake at 190°C/375°F/Mark 5 for 45 minutes. Test that rice and onions are cooked, then serve.

4 cod steaks
4 tomatoes, skinned and
   coarsely chopped
1 green pepper, deseeded and
   coarsely chopped
salt, pepper
¼-½ teaspoon chilli powder
2 onions, finely sliced
6 tablespoons rice

Flemish Fish

Cut the fish into serving portions if necessary and place in a buttered casserole dish. Sprinkle the onion over the fish. Add salt and pepper and nutmeg and just cover with cider and lemon juice. Slide the bay leaf and celery stick down the side of the fish. Cover and bake at 190°C/375°F/Mark 5 for 15 minutes. When cooked remove the bay leaf and celery and pour off the liquor into a small saucepan. Boil for 5 minutes to reduce. Add breadcrumbs and parsley and stir well. Heat through and pour over the fish. Serve at once.

750g/1½lb white fish (cod,
   haddock, coley or pollack)
1 small onion, finely chopped
salt, pepper, nutmeg
cider
juice 2 lemons
1 bay leaf
1 stick celery, trimmed
50g/2oz breadcrumbs
2 tablespoons chopped parsley

Aunty Mary's Fish Hot Pot

Poach the fish in a little stock and cut into chunks. Fry the onions in butter. Boil potatoes in lightly salted water and dice when cooked. Grease a casserole dish and layer potatoes, onions and fish, starting and ending with potatoes and sprinkling each layer with salt and pepper. Spoon on the cream and top with grated cheese. Bake at 220°C/425°F/Mark 7 for 10 minutes. If necessary, brown under the grill.

750g/1½lb white fish fillets
   (hake, haddock or huss)
stock
4 onions, sliced
25g/1oz butter
4 potatoes
salt, pepper
2 tablespoons cream
25g/1oz grated cheese

Shrimp and Pepper Omelette

Place shrimps or prawns in a pan with pimentos and butter and warm through. Do not allow to overheat or the shrimps will toughen. Beat eggs with the water and season. Pour the eggs into a hot buttered frying pan and cook quickly, stirring a little. When the omelette is almost cooked, sprinkle the shrimps and pimentos over the top and fold up. Serve at once.

225g/8oz peeled shrimps or
   prawns
75g/3oz canned or bottled
   pimentos, chopped
15g/½oz butter
7 eggs
1 tablespoon water
salt, pepper

Mushroom Fish Pie

450g/1lb potatoes
butter
milk
salt, pepper
350g/12oz white fish (cod,
  coley or haddock)
200g/7oz canned tuna, drained
100g/4oz peeled prawns
100g/4oz mushrooms, sliced
300g/10oz canned condensed
  mushroom soup
juice ½ lemon
25g/1oz grated cheese

Boil the potatoes until cooked and mash with butter and milk. Season to taste. Poach the white fish in a little water until tender. Remove any bones or skin and flake. Flake the tuna. Mix white fish, tuna and prawns in a casserole dish. Place the mushrooms on top of the fish. Pour over the condensed soup and add lemon juice and seasoning. Cover with mashed potatoes and fork the top. Sprinkle with grated cheese and bake at 190°C/375°F/ Mark 5 for 30-35 minutes until browned on top.

Egg and Anchovy Platter

4 large tomatoes, skinned and
  sliced
6 hard-boiled eggs, sliced
2 cartons potted shrimps
80ml/3floz mayonnaise
  (page 66)
1 teaspoon anchovy essence
sprigs watercress
200g/7oz canned sweetcorn,
  drained
4-6 canned anchovy fillets,
  soaked and drained

Arrange the tomatoes on a large plate and place hard-boiled eggs on top, leaving the outer ring of tomatoes clear. Sprinkle the potted shrimps and their butter over the eggs. Next mix the mayonnaise with anchovy essence and spoon on top. Decorate the outside with sprigs of watercress and small mounds of sweetcorn and arrange anchovies in curls across the centre.

Prawn and Herb Vol-au-vents

50g/2oz butter
4 tablespoons flour
750ml/1¼pints milk
450g/1lb peeled prawns
2 teaspoons dried marjoram
1 teaspoon dried dill
salt, pepper
8 large baked vol-au-vent cases
lemon wedges
sprigs parsley

Melt the butter in a pan and stir in the flour. Add the milk, stirring all the time, and bring to the boil. Continue cooking for 2-3 minutes. Add prawns and herbs and season to taste. Heat through and pile into the vol-au-vent cases. Serve garnished with lemon wedges and parsley.

Index